W9-ATC-307

STIR-FRIES
BEST-EVER WOK AND PAN RECIPES

STIR-FRIES
BEST-EVER WOK AND PAN RECIPES

bay books

INDEX OF RECIPES

STIR-FRY BASICS

Once the ingredients are prepared, the secret of stir-frying is to cook quickly over high heat and keep the food moving constantly around the wok.

Stir-frying is a fast, relatively healthy way to cook food. It involves quick cooking where the food is tossed around in a wok over high heat in a minimum amount of oil (although we have also included some recipes that combine initial stir-frying of ingredients with a short simmer to produce typical Asian curries). Preparation of ingredients is essential because once you start to cook there is no time to chop anything extra or hunt through cupboards.

OILS

For stir-frying, use oils that have a high smoking point. These include canola oil and peanut oil. Olive oil may be used to add flavour to warm stir-fry salads. If you are trying to cut down on fat, use an oil spray.

INGREDIENTS

MEAT AND POULTRY Meat to be stir-fried needs to be from a cut which will be tender after only a short cooking time. It should be cut across the grain into strips or small pieces so that it cooks quickly and evenly. Use chicken breast or thigh. Marinating meat or chicken helps to tenderize it and allows flavours to permeate the meat. Make sure the marinade is drained well before stir-frying, otherwise the meat or chicken will tend to steam rather than fry.

SEAFOOD Quick cooking suits seafood perfectly. Squid, prawns and scallops need the briefest possible time in the wok until they are cooked through. Use firm-fleshed fish so it can be stir-fried without breaking up.

VEGETABLES Stir-frying affects different vegetables in different ways. The intense heat caramelizes their sugar, but retains most of their vitamins and colour. Vegetables such as cauliflower, potatoes and carrots require a slightly longer cooking time and should be cut into small pieces or thin strips, whereas peas, asparagus and mushrooms should be cooked quickly at the end. Bean sprouts, herbs and greens, such as bok choy and spinach, should be added for the final minute or so, but for no longer because they will wilt quickly.

WOKS

There are many different types of wok available. The traditional basic wok is made of carbon steel. In its modern form the wok comes made of copper, stainless steel, cast iron and non-stick materials. Buy the heaviest wok you can find as it will retain heat well without scorching. You can also buy electric woks—these are non-stick and are kept at a constant high heat by an electric element.

The shape of a wok should be wide with deep, sloping sides and a round or wide, flattish bottom. It should be about 30–35 cm (12–14 inches) in diameter as small amounts of food can be cooked easily enough in a large wok but not vice versa. Flat-bottomed woks work well on electric stovetops as they sit directly on the hotplate—a wok ring often holds the wok too far away from the heat source for successful stir-frying. Some of the more modern stovetops have a special wide gas burner for woks.

Wok lids are important as they can be used to form a seal for a couple of minutes to steam any slower cooking ingredients or greens. Many recipes will instruct you to cover the wok for a short time at the end of cooking.

If you do not have a wok, you can use a large heavy-based frying pan for stir-frying, but you will need to cook the food in smaller batches to prevent it stewing.

SEASONING THE WOK

Steel woks come with an oily film which needs to be scrubbed off with hot water and detergent before use. The wok should then be dried off and heated over high heat. When it starts to become hot, brush it with vegetable oil, remove it from the heat and wipe it dry with a paper towel (it will blacken as you season it). Repeat this step several times to season the wok. As you use the wok, the seasoned layer (wok hay) will build up, turning darker and darker and adding flavour to the food.

A properly seasoned or a non-stick wok shouldn't be cleaned by scouring with an abrasive material like steel wool. Each time, after you have finished cooking and your wok has cooled down, simply wash it with hot water and a soft brush or cloth. Make sure you dry it throroughly over heat before storing in a dry area, otherwise it will rust. If you have a steel wok you should wipe or brush the inside with a very thin layer of oil before putting it away. This will keep it in good condition. Electric woks should also be rinsed in hot water, dried very thoroughly and coated with a thin film of oil after use.

The outside of the wok may occasionally need a good clean. Try not to used detergents—they damage the seasoning. If you do burn a stir-fry, you may need to use detergent and even a fine steel wool to clean the wok and may need to re-season.

WOK TOOLS

Utensils needed to stir-fry are minimal—a sharp knife for preparation and a wok turner or charn. This is a spade-like scoop, ideal for the continuous scooping and turning required. Flat spatulas also work well because they move the food around easily and follow the curvature of the wok.

Only wooden or plastic utensils should be used on non-stick woks so that the surface is not scratched.

TYPES OF WOKS

You can buy electric woks that are non-stick and are kept at a high heat by an element.

The oily film on a new wok has to be scrubbed off before use.

A wok will blacken as you season it and turn darker as you use it.

WARM CITRUS BEEF SALAD

oil, for cooking

500 g (1 lb) rump or sirloin steak, cut into thin strips

1 onion, sliced

2 cloves garlic, crushed

1 teaspoon grated fresh ginger

1 teaspoon grated lemon rind

1 teaspoon grated orange rind

1 tablespoon lemon juice

1 tablespoon orange juice

100 g (3½ oz) rocket leaves

40 g (1¼ oz) snow pea sprouts (mangetout)

1 lemon, segmented

1 orange, segmented

1   Heat the wok until very hot, add 1 tablespoon of the oil and swirl it around to coat the side. Stir-fry the beef in batches until well browned, adding more oil when necessary. Remove all the beef from the wok and set aside.

2   Reheat the wok, add 1 tablespoon of the oil and stir-fry the onion, garlic and ginger for 3–4 minutes, or until tender. Return the meat to the wok along with the combined lemon and orange rind and juice.

3   Bring to the boil, then toss the rocket through the beef mixture and cook until the rocket is just wilted. Serve immediately on a bed of snow pea sprouts, surrounded by the lemon and orange segments.

INGREDIENTS

oil, for cooking
500 g (1 lb) round steak, cut into thin strips
2 cloves garlic, crushed
1 onion, sliced
300 g (10 oz) sugar snap peas
2 tablespoons honey
2 teaspoons soy sauce
2 tablespoons oyster sauce
3 teaspoons cracked black pepper

1 Heat the wok until very hot, add 1 tablespoon of the oil and swirl it around to coat the side. Stir-fry the beef in batches over high heat. Remove and drain on paper towels.

2 Reheat the wok, add 1 tablespoon of the oil and stir-fry the garlic, onion and sugar snap peas until softened. Remove from the wok and set aside.

3 Add the honey, soy sauce, oyster sauce and cracked pepper to the wok. Bring to the boil, then reduce the heat and simmer for 3–4 minutes, or until the sauce thickens slightly.

4 Increase the heat, return the meat and vegetables to the wok, and toss for 2–3 minutes, or until well combined and heated through.

MARINATED LEMON GRASS BEEF

INGREDIENTS

500 g (1 lb) rump steak, cut into thin strips
3 stems lemon grass, white part only, finely chopped
1 onion, finely chopped
3 cloves garlic, finely chopped
2 tablespoons fish sauce
2 teaspoons sugar
1 tablespoon oil
¼ cup (40 g/1¼ oz) chopped roasted peanuts

1 Put the steak in a large glass or ceramic bowl. Mix the lemon grass, onion, garlic, fish sauce, sugar and oil to make a marinade. Pour over the meat and toss well. Cover and refrigerate for 3–4 hours.

2 Heat the wok until very hot and stir-fry the beef in two batches over high heat until it is just browned. Toss constantly to make sure the small pieces of onion and lemon grass don't catch on the wok and burn.

3 Return all the meat to the wok. Add the roasted peanuts and toss quickly until combined. Serve immediately.

INGREDIENTS

500 g (1 lb) rump steak, cut into thin strips
1 tablespoon cornflour (cornstarch)
2 tablespoons sherry
2 tablespoons soy sauce
2 teaspoons sugar
oil, for cooking
1 onion, thinly sliced
2 cloves garlic, finely chopped
1 tablespoon finely chopped fresh ginger
1 red capsicum (pepper), thinly sliced
90 g (3 oz) drained bamboo shoots, sliced
6 spring onions, diagonally sliced
2 tablespoons salted black beans, rinsed well and mashed

1   Put the beef in a glass or ceramic bowl. Combine the cornflour with the sherry, soy sauce and sugar to make a marinade. Pour over the meat and toss well. Cover and refrigerate for 30 minutes.

2   Drain the meat, reserving the marinade. Heat the wok until very hot, add 2 teaspoons of the oil and swirl it around to coat the side. Stir-fry the meat in two batches for 2–3 minutes, or until browned and just cooked. Add more oil when necessary. Remove all the meat from the wok.

3   Reheat the wok, add 1 tablespoon of oil and stir-fry the onion over medium heat for 3–4 minutes, or until softened. Stir in the garlic, ginger and capsicum, then increase the heat to high and cook for 2–3 minutes, or until the capsicum is just tender.

4   Add the reserved marinade, bamboo shoots, spring onion, black beans and 2–3 table-spoons water to the wok. Toss over high heat until the ingredients are well coated and the sauce is boiling. Return the beef to the wok and toss until heated through. Remove from the heat and season well. Serve immediately.

CORIANDER BEEF

500 g (1 lb) rump steak, cut into thin strips
4 cloves garlic, finely chopped
1 tablespoon finely chopped fresh ginger
½ cup (25 g/¾ oz) chopped coriander (cilantro) roots, stems and leaves
¼ cup (60 ml/2 fl oz) oil
oil, extra, for cooking
2 red onions, thinly sliced
½ red capsicum (pepper), thinly sliced
½ green capsicum (pepper), thinly sliced
1 tablespoon lime juice
½ cup (25 g/¾ oz) chopped coriander (cilantro) leaves, extra

1 Place the beef strips in a glass or ceramic bowl. Add the garlic, ginger, coriander and oil. Mix together well, then cover and refrigerate for 1–2 hours.

2 Heat the wok until very hot and stir-fry the meat in three batches over high heat for 2–3 minutes, or until the meat is just cooked. Remove all the meat from the wok and keep it warm.

3 Heat 1 tablespoon oil, add the onion and cook over medium-high heat for 3–4 minutes, or until the onion is slightly softened. Add the capsicum, and cook, tossing constantly, for 3–4 minutes, or until the capsicum is slightly softened.

4 Return all the meat to the wok with the lime juice and extra coriander. Toss well, then remove from the heat and season well with salt and cracked black pepper. Serve immediately.

INGREDIENTS

250 g (8 oz) instant noodles
500 g (1 lb) beef, thinly sliced
2 teaspoons sesame oil
2 cloves garlic, crushed
1 tablespoon grated fresh ginger
oil, for cooking
6 spring onions, sliced on the diagonal
1 small red capsicum (pepper), thinly sliced
125 g (4 oz) snow peas (mangetout), halved on the diagonal
4 tablespoons black bean and garlic sauce (see note)
2 tablespoons hoisin sauce
$^1/_2$ cup (60 g/2 oz) bean sprouts

1 Cook the noodles according to the manufacturer's directions, then drain and keep warm.

2 Place the beef, sesame oil, garlic and ginger in a bowl and mix together well. Heat the wok until very hot, add 1 tablespoon of the oil and swirl it around to coat the side. Add half the beef and stir-fry for 2–3 minutes, or until the beef is just cooked. Remove from the wok, add a little more oil and cook the rest of the beef. Remove all the beef from the wok

3 Heat 1 tablespoon oil in the wok. Add the spring onion, capsicum and snow peas and stir-fry for 2 minutes. Return the beef to the wok and stir in the black bean and garlic sauce, hoisin sauce and 1 tablespoon water.

4 Add the noodles to the wok and toss to heat through. Serve immediately, topped with bean sprouts.

NOTE Black bean and garlic sauce is available at Asian grocery stores or good supermarkets.

ASIAN PEPPERED BEEF

INGREDIENTS

600 g (1¼ lb) skirt steak, thinly sliced
2 cloves garlic, finely chopped
2 teaspoons finely chopped fresh ginger
2 onions, thinly sliced
2 tablespoons Chinese rice wine
1 teaspoon sesame oil
1 tablespoon soy sauce
1 tablespoon oyster sauce
2 teaspoons sugar
1 teaspoon Sichuan peppercorns, crushed
1 tablespoon black peppercorns, crushed
2 spring onions, chopped into 2.5 cm (1 inch) lengths
oil, for cooking

1 Place the beef strips in a large bowl. Add the garlic, ginger, onion, rice wine, sesame oil, soy sauce, oyster sauce, sugar and peppercorns, and mix together well. Cover and marinate in the refrigerator for at least 2 hours.

2 Drain, discarding any excess liquid, and stir in the spring onion.

3 Heat the wok until very hot, add 1 tablespoon of the oil and swirl it around to coat the side. Add half the beef and stir-fry for 6 minutes, or until seared and cooked to your liking. Repeat with the rest of the beef. Serve immediately.

NOTE The wok needs to be searing hot for this recipe. The beef is easier to thinly slice if you put it in the freezer for half an hour beforehand.

INGREDIENTS

oil, for cooking
500 g (1 lb) beef fillet or lean rump, thinly sliced
2 cloves garlic, crushed
¼ cup finely chopped coriander (cilantro) roots and stems
1 tablespoon grated palm sugar
⅓ cup (80 ml/2¾ fl oz) lime juice
2 tablespoons fish sauce
2 small red chillies, seeded, finely sliced
2 red Asian shallots, finely sliced
2 telegraph cucumbers, sliced into thin ribbons
1 cup (30 g/1 oz) mint leaves
1 cup (90 g/3 oz) bean sprouts
¼ cup (30 g/1 oz) chopped roasted peanuts

1   Heat the wok until very hot, add 1 tablespoon of the oil and swirl it around to coat the side. Add half the beef and cook for 1–2 minutes, or until medium rare. Remove from the wok and set aside. Repeat with the rest of the beef.

2   Place the garlic, coriander, palm sugar, lime juice, fish sauce, ¼ teaspoon ground white pepper and ¼ teaspoon salt in a bowl, and stir until all the sugar has dissolved. Add the chilli and shallots and mix well.

3   Pour the sauce over the beef while still hot, mix well, then cool to room temperature.

4   In a separate bowl, toss together the cucumber and mint leaves, and refrigerate until required.

5   Place the cucumber and mint on a serving platter, and top with the beef, bean sprouts and roasted peanuts. Serve immediately.

BEEF WITH BOK CHOY

INGREDIENTS

1 bunch bok choy
oil, for cooking
2 cloves garlic, crushed
250 g (8 oz) rump steak, thinly sliced
2 tablespoons soy sauce
1 tablespoon sweet sherry
2 tablespoons chopped basil
2 teaspoons sesame oil

1   Wash the bok choy and drain. Cut the leaves into wide strips and the stems into thin strips. Heat the wok until very hot, add 1 tablespoon of the oil and swirl to coat the side. Add the garlic and stir-fry for 30 seconds.

2   Add another tablespoon of oil to the wok and add the meat in batches. Stir-fry for 3 minutes over high heat until the meat has browned but not cooked through. Remove from the wok.

3   Add the bok choy to the wok and stir-fry for 30 seconds or until just wilted. Add the meat, soy sauce and sherry. Stir-fry for 2–3 minutes or until the meat is tender.

4   Add the basil and sesame oil and toss well. Serve immediately.

INGREDIENTS

500 g (1 lb) rump steak
1 tablespoon peanut oil
2 tablespoons oyster sauce
2 teaspoons mild curry powder
1 tablespoon soft brown sugar
1 small Lebanese cucumber, thinly sliced
1 red onion, sliced
1 red capsicum (pepper), cut into thin strips
1 small red chilli, seeded and chopped
¼ cup (15 g/½ oz) chopped mint
⅓ cup (60 g/2 oz) chopped unsalted peanuts or cashews
500 g (1 lb) Hokkien noodles

Dressing
½ cup (125 ml/4 fl oz) rice vinegar
2 tablespoons fish sauce
¼ cup (60 g/2 oz) caster sugar
2 teaspoons finely chopped fresh ginger
1 small red chilli, seeded and chopped
1 tablespoon chopped coriander (cilantro) leaves

1 Remove all visible fat from the meat. Combine the peanut oil, oyster sauce, curry powder and brown sugar in a small bowl.

2 Heat a wok over medium heat. Add the steak and cook for 6 8 minutes, turning and basting with half the sauce during cooking. Remove the steak from the wok.

3 To make the dressing, whisk together all the ingredients.

4 Place the cucumber, onion, capsicum and chilli in a large bowl. Add the mint and nuts. Thinly slice the meat, add to the bowl with the dressing and lightly toss to combine. If you have time, leave for a few minutes to marinate.

5 Place the noodles in the same wok and stir-fry over medium heat for 1–2 minutes. Stir in the remaining basting sauce and toss until heated through. Divide the noodles among serving bowls and top with the salad. Serve immediately.

QUICK BEEF AND NOODLE SALAD

SPICY SAUSAGE STIR-FRY

INGREDIENTS

2 tablespoons oil
500 g (1 lb) potato, cubed
500 g (1 lb) orange sweet potato (kumera), cubed
6 chorizo sausages, diagonally sliced
2 cloves garlic, thinly sliced
1 red onion, cut into wedges
200 g (6½ oz) broccoli, chopped
1 red capsicum (pepper), cut into short thick strips
½ cup (125 ml/4 fl oz) tomato paste (purée)
2 tablespoons chopped fresh parsley

1 Heat the wok until very hot, add the oil and swirl it around to coat the side. Stir-fry the potato and sweet potato over medium heat until tender and golden. Remove and drain on paper towels, then place on a serving plate and cover to keep warm.

2 Add the sausage to the wok and stir-fry in batches over high heat for 3–4 minutes, or until crisp. Remove and drain on paper towels.

3 Add the garlic and onion to the wok and stir-fry for 2 minutes, or until the onion softens. Add the broccoli and capsicum, and stir-fry for 1 minute. Return the sausage to the wok, add the tomato purée and toss to combine. Add the parsley and season with salt and black pepper. Toss well and serve on top of the stir-fried potato.

INGREDIENTS

1 tablespoon oil
1 large onion, thinly sliced
2 carrots, cut into matchsticks
200 g (6½ oz) broccoli, chopped
6 spring onions, diagonally sliced
1 tablespoon finely chopped fresh ginger
3 cloves garlic, finely chopped
400 g (13 oz) Chinese barbecued pork, thinly sliced
2 tablespoons soy sauce
2 tablespoons mirin
2 cups (180 g/6 oz) bean sprouts

1 Heat the wok until very hot, add the oil and swirl it around to coat the side. Stir-fry the onion over medium heat for 3–4 minutes, or until slightly softened. Add the carrot, broccoli, spring onion, ginger and garlic and cook for 4–5 minutes, tossing the mixture constantly.

2 Increase the heat to high and add the barbecued pork. Toss constantly until the pork is well mixed with the vegetables and is heated through. Add the soy sauce and mirin, and toss until the ingredients are well coated. (The wok should be hot enough for the sauce to reduce into a glaze.) Add the bean sprouts and season well with salt and pepper. Serve immediately.

BARBECUED PORK AND BROCCOLI

INGREDIENTS

2 tablespoons oil
375 g (12 oz) pork fillet, thinly sliced
2 small red chillies, seeded and finely chopped
6 spring onions, chopped
1 tablespoon mild curry paste
2 tablespoons fish sauce
1–2 tablespoons lime juice
2 teaspoons crushed palm sugar
2 teaspoons cornflour (cornstarch)
½–1 teaspoon seasoning sauce
⅓ cup (50 g/1¾ oz) roasted unsalted cashews
shredded lime rind, to garnish

1   Heat the wok until very hot, add the oil and swirl it around to coat the side. Stir-fry the pork slices, chilli and spring onion in batches over high heat for 2 minutes, or until the pork just changes colour. Stir in the curry paste and stir-fry for 1 minute. Remove from the wok and set aside.

2   Combine the fish sauce, lime juice, sugar and cornflour with ½ cup (125 ml/4 fl oz) water. Pour into the wok and stir for 1 minute, or until heated through and slightly thickened. Return the meat to the wok and toss until heated through.

3   Stir in the seasoning sauce, to taste, and cashews. Top with the lime rind.

INGREDIENTS

400 g (13 oz) lean pork leg steaks
1 tablespoon canned salted black beans, rinsed
500 g (1 lb) baby bok choy
2 teaspoons sesame oil
2 onions, finely sliced
2 cloves garlic, finely chopped
2–3 teaspoons chopped ginger
1 red capsicum (pepper), cut into strips
¼ cup (90 g/3 oz) water chestnuts, finely sliced
2 tablespoons oyster sauce
1 tablespoon soy sauce
2 teaspoons fish sauce

1 Slice the pork steaks into strips, cutting across the grain. Roughly chop the beans. Separate the leaves of the bok choy, trim away the tough ends and shred the leaves.

2 Heat half the sesame oil in a large wok. Cook the onion, garlic and ginger over high heat for 3–4 minutes, add the capsicum and cook for 2–3 minutes. Remove from the wok. Heat the remaining sesame oil and stir-fry the pork in batches over high heat.

3 Return all the pork to the wok along with the onion mixture, black beans, shredded bok choy, water chestnuts and oyster, soy and fish sauces. Toss quickly to combine the ingredients, lower the heat, cover and steam for 3–4 minutes, or until the bok choy has just wilted. Serve immediately.

BLACK BEAN PORK WITH BOK CHOY

PORK AND GREEN BEANS WITH GINGER SAUCE

³/₄ cup (185 ml/6 fl oz) soy sauce
4 tablespoons white or rice wine vinegar
1 teaspoon sugar
pinch of dried chilli flakes
3 teaspoons cornflour (cornstarch)
600 g (1¹/₄ lb) pork fillet, trimmed and cut into thin slices
2 tablespoons peanut oil
350 g (11 oz) green beans, cut into short lengths
2 cloves garlic, chopped
2 tablespoons grated fresh ginger

1   Place the soy sauce, vinegar, sugar, chilli flakes, cornflour and ¹/₃ cup (80 ml/2³/₄ fl oz) water in a bowl and mix well. Add the pork and toss to coat well.

2   Heat a wok over high heat, add half the oil and swirl to coat the side. Drain the pork, reserving the liquid, and add to the wok. Stir-fry over high heat for 1–2 minutes, or until brown. Remove the pork from the wok.

3   Heat the remaining oil, add the beans and stir-fry for 3–4 minutes. Add the garlic and ginger and stir-fry for 1 minute, or until fragrant. Return the pork and any juices to the pan and add the reserved marinade. Bring to the boil and cook, stirring, for 1–2 minutes, or until slightly thickened. Serve with steamed rice.

NOTE   Rice wine vinegar is made by oxidising beer or wine made from fermented rice starch.

INGREDIENTS

2 tablespoons ghee (see note) or oil
1 onion, finely chopped
½ red capsicum (pepper), finely chopped
10 spring onions, thinly sliced
2–3 small red chillies, seeded and finely chopped
2–3 cloves garlic, finely chopped
1 tablespoon grated fresh ginger
125 g (4 oz) Chinese barbecued pork, finely chopped
6 eggs, lightly beaten
4 cups (740 g/1½ lb) cold cooked jasmine rice
1–2 teaspoons seasoning sauce
⅓ cup (20 g/¾ oz) chopped coriander (cilantro)
onion flakes, to garnish

1 Heat the wok until very hot, add the ghee and swirl it around to coat the side. Stir-fry the onion, capsicum, spring onion, chilli, garlic and ginger over medium-high heat for 2–3 minutes, or until the vegetables are cooked but not brown. Add the barbecued pork and toss to combine.

2 Reduce the heat, then pour in the beaten eggs. Season well with salt and pepper. Gently stir the egg mixture until it is creamy and almost set. Add the rice and gently stir-fry to incorporate all the ingredients and heat the mixture through.

3 Sprinkle with the seasoning sauce and stir in the coriander. Serve the savoury rice immediately, sprinkled with onion flakes.

NOTE Ghee is a form of clarified butter. It is the main type of fat used in Indian cooking and is available in most supermarkets.

INGREDIENTS

150 g (5 oz) dried rice vermicelli
oil, for cooking
250 g (8 oz) Chinese barbecued pork, cut into small pieces
250 g (8 oz) peeled raw prawns (shrimp), cut into small pieces
2 tablespoons Madras curry powder
2 cloves garlic, crushed
100 g (3½ oz) shiitake mushrooms, thinly sliced
1 onion, thinly sliced
100 g (3½ oz) green beans, thinly sliced on the diagonal
1 tablespoon soy sauce
4 spring onions, thinly sliced on the diagonal

1   Place the vermicelli in a large bowl, cover with boiling water and soak for 5 minutes. Drain well and spread out on a clean tea towel to dry.

2   Heat the wok until very hot, add 1 tablespoon of the oil and swirl it around to coat the side. Stir-fry the barbecued pork and the prawn pieces in batches over high heat. Remove from the wok and set aside.

3   Reheat the wok, add 2 tablespoons of the oil and stir-fry the curry powder and garlic for 1–2 minutes, or until fragrant. Add the mushrooms and onion and stir-fry over medium heat for 2–3 minutes, or until the onion and mushrooms are soft.

4   Return the pork and prawns to the wok, add the beans and 2 teaspoons water, and toss to combine. Add the drained noodles, soy sauce and spring onion. Toss well and serve.

INGREDIENTS

1 tablespoon oil
150 g (5 oz) pork loin, thinly sliced
5 spring onions, cut into short lengths
1 carrot, cut into thin strips
200 g (6^1/$_2$ oz) Chinese cabbage, shredded
500 g (1 lb) Hokkien noodles, gently pulled apart to separate
2 tablespoons shoshoyu
1 tablespoon Worcestershire sauce
1 tablespoon mirin
2 teaspoons caster sugar
1 cup (90 g/3 oz) bean sprouts, scraggly ends removed
1 sheet toasted nori, shredded

1   Heat the oil in a large wok over medium heat. Stir-fry the pork, spring onion and carrot for 1–2 minutes, or until the pork just changes colour.

2   Add the cabbage, noodles, shoshoyu, Worcestershire sauce, mirin, sugar and 2 tablespoons water. Cover and cook for 1 minute.

3   Add the bean sprouts and toss well to coat the vegetables and noodles in the sauce. Serve immediately, sprinkled with the shredded nori.

JAPANESE FRIED PORK AND NOODLES

INGREDIENTS

1.6 kg (3¹/₄ lb) Chinese broccoli, cut into short lengths
1 tablespoon peanut oil
2.5 cm (1 inch) piece fresh ginger, julienned
2 cloves garlic, crushed
500 g (1 lb) Chinese barbecue pork, thinly sliced
¹/₄ cup (60 ml/2 fl oz) chicken or vegetable stock
¹/₄ cup (60 ml/2 fl oz) oyster sauce
1 tablespoon kecap manis

1 Place the broccoli in a steamer over a wok of simmering water and cook for 5 minutes, or until just tender but still crisp.

2 Drain the wok, dry thoroughly and heat until very hot. Add the oil and swirl to coat. Add the ginger and garlic and stir-fry for 30 seconds, or until fragrant. Add the broccoli and pork and toss to coat.

3 Mix together the stock, oyster sauce and kecap manis and add to the wok. Toss thoroughly until heated through and then serve immediately.

INGREDIENTS

1¹/₂ tablespoons cornflour (cornstarch)
1 tablespoon Sichuan peppercorns, ground
2 egg whites, beaten
500 g (1 lb) pork fillet, thinly sliced
2 tablespoons peanut oil, plus 1 teaspoon, extra
1 red capsicum (pepper), thinly sliced
2 spring onions, sliced into short lengths
2 teaspoons chilli oil
4 star anise
2 cloves garlic, crushed
2 teaspoons finely chopped fresh ginger
2 tablespoons oyster sauce
2 tablespoons Chinese rice wine
2 tablespoons soy sauce
¹/₂ teaspoon sesame oil
2 teaspoons sugar

1   Place the cornflour, peppercorns, egg whites and ¹/₂ teaspoon salt in a bowl. Mix well, then add the pork and toss to coat.

2   Heat a wok until very hot, add 1 teaspoon peanut oil and swirl to coat the base and side of the wok with oil. Add the capsicum and spring onion and stir-fry for 1 minute. Remove from the wok.

3   Add 1 tablespoon peanut oil to the wok and swirl to coat the base and side of the wok. Add half the pork and stir-fry for 2 minutes, or until sealed. Remove. Repeat with the remaining oil and pork.

4   Add the chilli oil to the wok and swirl to coat. Add the star anise and stir-fry for 30 seconds, then add the garlic and ginger and stir-fry for another few seconds.

5   Combine the oyster sauce, rice wine, soy sauce, sesame oil and sugar, add to the wok and cook for 30 seconds. Return the pork to the wok and stir-fry for 1 minute, then stir in the vegetables and serve.

INDIAN LAMB AND SPINACH

2 cloves garlic, finely chopped
1 tablespoon finely chopped fresh ginger
$1/2$ teaspoon salt
1 tablespoon ground cumin
1 tablespoon ground coriander (cilantro)
1 teaspoon ground cinnamon
$1/2$ teaspoon ground allspice
$1/4$ cup (60 ml/2 fl oz) oil
600 g ($1^1/_4$ lb) lamb fillet, sliced diagonally
oil, for cooking
2 onions, thinly sliced
500 g (1 lb) English spinach, shredded
1 tablespoon lime juice
2 tablespoons toasted pine nuts

1   Combine the garlic, ginger, salt, spices and oil in a shallow glass or ceramic bowl. Add the sliced lamb and mix until well combined. Cover and refrigerate for at least 2 hours.

2   Heat the wok until very hot, and stir-fry the lamb in three batches over high heat for 2–3 minutes, or until the lamb is golden brown and just cooked. Remove the lamb from the wok and cover to keep warm.

3   Reheat the wok and add 1 tablespoon of the oil. Stir-fry the sliced onion over medium-high heat for 2–3 minutes, or until slightly softened. Add the spinach, cover and steam for 1–2 minutes, or until the spinach has just wilted. Return all the lamb and juices to the wok along with the lime juice and toasted pine nuts. Toss until thoroughly combined and season well with salt and pepper. Serve immediately.

INGREDIENTS

2 cups (40 g/1¼ oz) mint leaves
2 cloves garlic
¼ cup (40 g/1¼ oz) toasted pine nuts
½ cup (50 g/1¾ oz) grated Parmesan
¼ cup (60 ml/2 fl oz) olive oil
oil, for cooking
500 g (1 lb) lamb fillet, thinly sliced
1 onion, sliced
300 g (10 oz) mixed mushrooms, such as enoki, oyster, button, shimeji or Swiss brown

1 Place the mint, garlic, pine nuts and Parmesan in a food processor, and process for 10 seconds, or until finely chopped. With the motor running, gradually add the olive oil to form a paste. Season well.

2 Heat the wok until very hot, add 1 tablespoon of the oil and stir-fry the lamb in batches over medium-high heat until well browned. Remove all the lamb from the wok.

3 Reheat the wok, add 1 tablespoon of the oil and stir-fry the onion for 3–4 minutes, or until tender. Add the mushrooms and cook for 2 minutes.

4 Stir in the mint pesto. Return the lamb to the wok and toss over high heat for 5 minutes, or until the mushrooms are soft and the lamb is heated through. Season well.

INGREDIENTS

1 tablespoon peanut oil
500 g (^{1}/$_2$ lb) minced (ground) pork
2 garlic cloves, finely chopped
1 stalk lemon grass, finely chopped
2–3 red Asian shallots, thinly sliced
3 teaspoons finely grated fresh ginger
1 small red chilli, finely chopped
5 fresh kaffir lime (makrut) leaves, very finely shredded
170 g (6 oz) glass (mung bean) noodles
60 g (2 oz) baby English spinach leaves
50 g (1 cup/1^3/$_4$ oz) roughly chopped coriander
170 g (6 oz) peeled, finely chopped fresh pineapple
10 g (^{1}/$_2$ cup) mint leaves
1^1/$_2$ tablespoons shaved palm sugar or soft brown sugar
2 tablespoons fish sauce
80 ml (^{1}/$_3$ cup) lime juice
2 teaspoons sesame oil
2 teaspoons peanut oil, extra

1   Heat a wok until very hot, add the peanut oil and swirl to coat the wok. Add the pork and stir-fry in batches over high heat for 5 minutes, or until lightly golden. Add the garlic, lemon grass, shallots, grated ginger, chilli and lime leaves, and stir-fry for a further 1–2 minutes, or until fragrant.

2   Place the noodles in a large bowl and cover with boiling water for 30 seconds, or until softened. Rinse under cold water and drain well. Toss in a bowl with the spinach, coriander, pineapple, mint and pork mixture.

3   To make the dressing, mix together the palm sugar, fish sauce and lime juice. Add the sesame oil and extra peanut oil, and whisk to combine. Toss through the salad and season with freshly ground black pepper.

INGREDIENTS

2 tablespoons sesame seeds
1 tablespoon oil
2 teaspoons sesame oil
800 g (1 lb 10 oz) chicken tenderloins, cut diagonally into strips
1 leek, white part only, julienned
2 cloves garlic, crushed
2 tablespoons soy sauce
1 tablespoon mirin
1 teaspoon sugar

1   Heat a wok until very hot, add the sesame seeds and dry-fry over high heat until they are golden. Remove the seeds from the wok.

2   Reheat the wok, add the oils and swirl them around to coat the side. Stir-fry the chicken strips in three batches over high heat, tossing constantly until just cooked. Reheat the wok before each addition. Return all the chicken to the wok.

3   Add the julienned leek and the garlic and cook for 1–2 minutes, or until the leek is soft and golden. Check that the chicken is cooked through; if it is not cooked, reduce the heat and cook, covered, for 2 minutes, or until it is completely cooked.

4   Add the soy sauce, mirin, sugar and toasted sesame seeds to the wok, and toss well to combine. Season with salt and black pepper, and serve immediately. Delicious with pasta.

CHICKEN WITH WALNUTS AND STRAW MUSHROOMS

375 g (12 oz) chicken breast fillets or tenderloins, cut into thin strips
$1/2$ teaspoon five-spice powder
2 teaspoons cornflour (cornstarch)
2 tablespoons soy sauce
2 tablespoons oyster sauce
2 teaspoons soft brown sugar
1 teaspoon sesame oil
oil, for cooking
75 g ($2^1/_2$ oz) walnuts
150 g (5 oz) snake beans or green beans, chopped
6 spring onions, sliced
425 g (14 oz) can straw mushrooms, rinsed
230 g ($7^1/_2$ oz) can sliced bamboo shoots, rinsed

1 Dry the chicken strips with paper towels and sprinkle with the five-spice powder. Mix the cornflour with the soy sauce in a bowl until smooth. Add $1/2$ cup (125 ml/4 fl oz) water along with the oyster sauce, brown sugar and sesame oil.

2 Heat the wok until very hot, add 1 tablespoon of the oil and swirl it around to coat the side. Stir-fry the walnuts for 30 seconds, or until lightly browned. Drain on paper towels.

3 Reheat the wok over high heat. Add 1 tablespoon of the oil and stir-fry the chicken in batches for 2–3 minutes, or until just cooked through. Remove all of the chicken from the wok and set aside.

4 Add the snake beans, spring onion, straw mushrooms and bamboo shoots to the wok, and stir-fry for 2 minutes. Remove from the wok. Add the soy sauce mixture and heat for 1 minute, or until slightly thickened. Return the chicken and vegetables to the wok, and toss to coat with the sauce. Season well. Serve at once, sprinkled with the stir-fried walnuts.

INGREDIENTS

Chilli jam

10 dried long red chillies

4 tablespoons peanut oil

1 red capsicum (pepper), chopped

1 head (50 g/1³/₄ oz) garlic, peeled and roughly chopped

200 g (7 oz) red Asian shallots, chopped

100 g (3¹/₂ oz) palm sugar, grated, or soft brown sugar

2 tablespoons tamarind purée (see note)

1 tablespoon peanut oil

6 spring onions (scallions), cut into 3 cm (1¹/₄ inch) lengths

500 g (1 lb 2 oz) chicken breast fillet, cut into slices

50 g (¹/₃ cup) roasted unsalted cashews

1 tablespoon fish sauce

15 g (¹/₂ cup) Thai basil

1 To make the chilli jam, soak the chillies in a bowl of boiling water for 15 minutes. Drain, remove the seeds and chop. Put in a food processor, then add the oil, capsicum, garlic and shallots and blend until smooth.

2 Heat a wok over medium heat and add the chilli mixture. Cook, stirring occasionally, for 15 minutes. Add the sugar and tamarind and simmer for 10 minutes, or until it darkens and reaches a jam-like consistency. Remove from the wok.

3 Clean and reheat the wok over high heat, add the oil and swirl to coat. Stir-fry the spring onion for 1 minute, then add the chicken and stir-fry for 3–5 minutes, or until golden brown and tender. Stir in the cashews, fish sauce and 4 tablespoons of the chilli jam. Stir-fry for a further 2 minutes, then stir in the basil and serve.

NOTE Use a non-stick or stainless steel wok to cook this recipe because the tamarind purée will react with the metal in a regular wok and will taint the dish.

INGREDIENTS

500 g (1 lb) chicken thigh fillets, cut into strips
5 cm (2 inch) piece ginger, cut into paper-thin slices
4 spring onions, thinly sliced
oil, for cooking
1 red capsicum (pepper), thinly sliced
1 tablespoon mirin
1 tablespoon lime marmalade
2 teaspoons grated lime rind
2 tablespoons lime juice

1 Put the chicken, ginger, spring onion and some ground black pepper in a dish. Toss well to combine.

2 Heat a wok until very hot, add 1 tablespoon of the oil and swirl it around to coat the side. Stir-fry the chicken mixture in three batches over high heat for about 3 minutes, or until it is golden brown and cooked through. Reheat the wok in between each batch, adding more oil when necessary. Remove all the chicken from the wok and set aside.

3 Reheat the wok, add the capsicum and stir-fry for 30 seconds. Add the mirin, marmalade, lime rind and juice, and season with salt and freshly ground black pepper. Cover and steam for 1 minute. Add the chicken and cook, uncovered, for 2 minutes, or until heated through.

INGREDIENTS

1 tablespoon oil
750 g lamb fillet, thinly sliced (see note)
4 cloves garlic, finely chopped
2 small fresh red chillies, thinly sliced
1/3 cup (80 ml) oyster sauce
2 1/2 tablespoons fish sauce
1 1/2 teaspoons sugar
1/2 cup (25 g) chopped fresh mint
1/4 cup (5 g) whole fresh mint leaves

1 Heat a wok over high heat, add the oil and swirl to coat. Add the lamb and garlic in batches and stir-fry for 1–2 minutes, or until the lamb is almost cooked. Return all the lamb to the wok. Stir in the chilli, oyster sauce, fish sauce, sugar and the chopped mint leaves, and cook for another 1–2 minutes.

2 Remove from the heat, fold in the whole mint leaves and serve immediately with rice.

NOTE Make sure you slice the lamb across the grain—this will minimise the meat breaking up and shrinking when cooking.

STIR-FRIED LAMB WITH MINT AND CHILLI

NASI GORENG

INGREDIENTS

5–8 long red chillies, seeded and chopped
2 teaspoons shrimp paste
8 cloves garlic, finely chopped
oil, for cooking
2 eggs, lightly beaten
350 g (12 oz) chicken thigh fillets, cut into thin strips
200 g (6½ oz) peeled raw prawns (shrimp), deveined
8 cups (1.5 kg/3 lb) cold cooked rice (see note)
⅓ cup (80 ml/2¾ fl oz) kecap manis
⅓ cup (80 ml/2¾ fl oz) soy sauce
2 small Lebanese cucumbers, finely chopped
1 large tomato, finely chopped
lime wedges, to serve

1 Mix the chilli, shrimp paste and garlic to a paste in a food processor.

2 Heat the wok until very hot, add 1 tablespoon of the oil and swirl it around to coat the side. Add the beaten eggs and push the egg up the edges of the wok to form a large omelette. Cook for 1 minute over medium heat, or until the egg is set, then flip it over and cook the other side for 1 minute. Remove from the wok and cool before slicing into strips.

3 Reheat the wok, add 1 tablespoon of the oil and stir-fry the chicken and half the chilli paste over high heat until the chicken is just cooked. Remove the chicken from the wok.

4 Reheat the wok, add 1 tablespoon of the oil and stir-fry the prawns and the remaining chilli paste until cooked. Remove from the wok and set aside.

5 Reheat the wok, add 1 tablespoon of the oil and the rice, and toss over medium heat for 4–5 minutes to heat through. Add the kecap manis and soy sauce and toss constantly until all of the rice is coated in the sauces. Return the chicken and prawns to the wok, and toss to heat through. Season well. Transfer to a serving bowl and top with the omelette strips, cucumber and tomato. Serve with the lime wedges.

NOTE Rice should be refrigerated overnight before making fried rice to let the grains dry out and separate.

INGREDIENTS

100 g (3¹/₂ oz) dried rice vermicelli
oil, for cooking
500 g (1 lb) chicken breast fillets, cut into thin strips
2 cloves garlic, crushed
1 teaspoon grated fresh ginger
2 teaspoons Asian-style curry powder
1 red onion, sliced
1 red capsicum (pepper), cut into short strips
2 carrots, cut into matchsticks
2 zucchini (courgette), cut into matchsticks
1 tablespoon soy sauce

1   Place the vermicelli in a large bowl, cover with boiling water and soak for 5 minutes. Drain well and place on a tea towel to dry.

2   Heat the wok until very hot, add 1 tablespoon of the oil and swirl it around to coat the side. Stir-fry the chicken in batches over high heat until browned and tender. Remove all the chicken and drain on paper towels.

3   Reheat the wok, add 1 tablespoon of the oil and stir-fry the garlic, ginger, curry powder and onion for 1–2 minutes, or until fragrant. Add the capsicum, carrot and zucchini to the wok, and stir-fry until well coated in the spices. Add 1 tablespoon water and stir-fry for 1 minute.

4   Add the drained noodles and chicken to the wok. Add the soy sauce and toss using two wooden spoons until well combined. Season well with salt and serve.

INGREDIENTS

2 tablespoons vegetable oil

600 g (1 lb 5 oz) lean beef fillet, thinly sliced across the grain

1 large red onion, cut into wedges

1 red capsicum (pepper), thinly sliced

1¹/₂ tablespoons chilli garlic sauce

125 ml (¹/₂ cup) good-quality plum sauce

1 tablespoon light soy sauce

2 teaspoons rice vinegar

good pinch of finely ground white pepper

4 spring onions (scallions), sliced on the diagonal

1 Heat a wok over high heat, then add 1 tablespoon of the oil and swirl to coat the side of the wok. Stir-fry the beef in two batches for 2–3 minutes each batch, or until browned and just cooked. Remove from the wok.

2 Heat the remaining oil in the wok, add the onion and stir-fry for 1 minute before adding the capsicum and continuing to stir-fry for 2–3 minutes, or until just tender. Add the chilli garlic sauce and stir for 1 minute, then return the meat to the wok and add the plum sauce, soy sauce, rice vinegar, white pepper and most of the spring onion.

3 Toss everything together for 1 minute, or until the meat is reheated. Sprinkle with the remaining spring onion, then serve with steamed rice or noodles.

INGREDIENTS

6 baby bok choy

8 stems Chinese broccoli

150 g (5 oz) dried rice stick noodles

2 tablespoons oil

375 g (12 oz) chicken breast fillets or tenderloins, cut into
thin strips

2–3 cloves garlic, crushed

5 cm (2 inch) piece ginger, grated

6 spring onions, cut into short pieces

1 tablespoon sherry

1 cup (90 g/3 oz) bean sprouts

Sauce

2 teaspoons cornflour (cornstarch)

2 tablespoons soy sauce

2 tablespoons oyster sauce

2 teaspoons soft brown sugar

1 teaspoon sesame oil

1 Remove any tough outer leaves from the bok choy and Chinese broccoli. Cut into 4 cm (1½ inch) pieces across the leaves, including the stems. Wash well, then drain and dry thoroughly.

2 Place the rice stick noodles in a large heatproof bowl and cover with boiling water. Soak for 5–8 minutes, or until softened. Rinse, then drain. Cut into short lengths using scissors.

3 Meanwhile, to make the sauce, combine the cornflour and soy sauce in a small bowl. Mix to a smooth paste, then stir in the oyster sauce, brown sugar, sesame oil and ½ cup (125 ml/4 fl oz) water.

4 Heat a wok until very hot, add the oil and swirl it around to coat the side. Stir-fry the chicken strips, garlic, ginger and spring onion in batches over high heat for 3–4 minutes, or until the chicken is cooked. Remove from the wok and set aside.

5 Add the chopped bok choy, Chinese broccoli and sherry to the wok, cover and steam for 2 minutes, or until the vegetables are wilted. Remove from the wok and set aside. Add the sauce to the wok and stir until the sauce is glossy and slightly thickened. Return the chicken, vegetables, noodles and bean sprouts to the wok, and stir until well combined and heated through.

NOTE Broccoli and English spinach may be used as the greens.

NOODLES WITH CHICKEN AND FRESH BLACK BEANS

2 teaspoons salted black beans

oil, for cooking

2 teaspoons sesame oil

500 g (1 lb) chicken thigh fillets, cut into thin strips

3 cloves garlic, very thinly sliced

4 spring onions, chopped

1 teaspoon sugar

1 red capsicum (pepper), sliced

100 g (3½ oz) green beans, cut into short pieces

300 g (10 oz) Hokkien noodles

2 tablespoons oyster sauce

1 tablespoon soy sauce

1 Rinse the black beans in running water. Drain and roughly chop.

2 Heat a wok until very hot, add 1 tablespoon of oil and the sesame oil and swirl it around to coat the side. Stir-fry the chicken in three batches, until well browned, tossing regularly. Remove from the wok and set aside.

3 Reheat the wok, add 1 tablespoon of the oil and stir-fry the garlic and spring onion for 1 minute. Add the black beans, sugar, capsicum and green beans, and cook for 1 minute. Sprinkle with 2 tablespoons of water, cover and steam for 2 minutes.

4 Gently separate the noodles and add to the wok with the chicken, oyster sauce and soy sauce, and toss well to combine. Cook, covered, for about 2 minutes, or until the noodles are just softened.

INGREDIENTS

¹/₂ Chinese barbecued duck (about 500 g/1 lb), boned
1 tablespoon oil
12 spring onions, cut into short lengths
1 large carrot, cut into batons
1 tablespoon cornflour (cornstarch)
1 tablespoon honey
1 tablespoon sherry
1 tablespoon vinegar
¹/₄ cup (60 ml/2 fl oz) plum sauce
1 tablespoon soy sauce
12 Chinese barbecued duck pancakes, to serve

1 Remove and discard any excess fat and some of the skin from the duck. Cut the duck into bite-sized pieces. Heat the wok until very hot, add the duck pieces and cook over high heat for 3–4 minutes, or until the skin starts to become crispy. Remove the duck from the wok.

2 Reheat the wok, add the oil and swirl it around to coat the side. Stir-fry the spring onion and the carrot over medium heat for 3–4 minutes, or until the carrot has softened slightly. Combine the cornflour with the honey, sherry, vinegar, plum sauce and soy sauce. Increase the heat to high, return the duck to the wok and toss well. When the wok is very hot, add the sauce mixture and toss constantly for 2–3 minutes to coat the duck and vegetables. The sauce will begin to caramelize and reduce to form a glaze.

3 Remove the wok from the heat. Serve the stir-fried duck mixture with the pancakes, which have been steamed for 3–4 minutes or warmed in the microwave. Place a small portion of duck in the middle of each pancake, fold in the edges and roll up.

SINGAPORE PEPPER CRAB

INGREDIENTS

Stir-fry sauce
2 tablespoons dark soy sauce
2 tablespoons oyster sauce
1 tablespoon grated palm sugar or soft brown sugar

2 kg (4 lb 8 oz) blue swimmer crabs
1–2 tablespoons peanut oil
150 g (5^1/$_2$ oz) butter
2 tablespoons finely chopped garlic
1 tablespoon finely chopped ginger
1 small red chilli, seeded and finely chopped
1^1/$_2$ tablespoons ground black pepper
1 spring onion, green part only, thinly sliced on the diagonal

1 Mix the ingredients for the sauce in a small bowl or jug and set aside.

2 Wash the crabs well with a stiff brush. Pull back the apron and remove the top shell from each crab (it should come off easily). Remove the intestine and the grey feathery gills. Using a large sharp knife, cut the crab lengthways through the centre of the body to form two halves with the legs attached. Cut each half in half again, crossways. Crack the thicker part of the legs with the back of a heavy knife or crab crackers.

3 Heat a wok over high heat, add a little oil and swirl to coat. Add the crab in a few batches, stir-frying over very high heat for 4 minutes each batch, or until the shells turn bright orange, adding more oil if needed. Remove from the wok. Reduce the heat to medium-high, add the butter, garlic, ginger, chilli and pepper and stir-fry for 30 seconds, then add the stir-fry sauce and simmer for 1 minute, or until glossy.

4 Return the crab to the wok, cover, stirring every minute for 4 minutes, or until cooked. Sprinkle with the spring onion and serve with rice. Provide bowls of warm water with lemon slices for rinsing sticky fingers.

INGREDIENTS

1 Chinese barbecued duck (about 1 kg/2 lb), boned
1 tablespoon oil
1 onion, sliced
2 cloves garlic, crushed
2 teaspoons grated fresh ginger
1 tablespoon orange rind
$^2/_3$ cup (170 ml/5$^1/_2$ fl oz) orange juice
$^1/_4$ cup (60 ml/2 fl oz) chicken stock
2 teaspoons soft brown sugar
2 teaspoons cornflour (cornstarch)
1.5 kg (3 lb) baby bok choy, leaves separated
1 orange, segmented

1   Cut the duck meat into pieces. Reserve and thinly slice some crispy skin for garnish. Heat
    the wok until very hot, add the oil and swirl it around to coat the side. Stir-fry the onion for
    3 minutes, or until tender. Stir in the garlic and ginger for 1–2 minutes. Pour in the
    combined orange rind, juice, stock and sugar. Bring to the boil.

2   Mix the cornflour with a little water to form a paste. Pour into the wok, stirring until
    the mixture boils and thickens. Place the duck pieces in the sauce and simmer for
    1–2 minutes, or until heated through. Remove from the wok and keep warm.

3   Place the bok choy in the wok with 2 tablespoons water. Cover and steam until just wilted.
    Arrange on a serving plate, spoon the duck mixture over the top and garnish with the
    orange segments and the crispy duck skin.

GINGER CHICKEN WITH MUSHROOMS AND WHEAT NOODLES

4 dried Chinese mushrooms
2 teaspoons cornflour (cornstarch)
2 tablespoons soy sauce
2 tablespoons oyster sauce
1 tablespoon mirin or sweet sherry
200 g (6¹/₂ oz) dried wheat noodles
1 teaspoon sesame oil
oil, for cooking
2–3 cloves garlic, crushed
8 cm (3 inch) piece fresh ginger, cut into matchsticks
375 g (12 oz) chicken breast fillets or tenderloins, cut into thin strips
1 red onion, cut into thin wedges
6 spring onions, cut into short lengths
185 g (6 oz) small field mushrooms, thickly sliced
1 cup (90 g/3 oz) bean sprouts
¹/₃ cup (20 g/³/₄ oz) chopped mint

1   Place the dried mushrooms in a small bowl and cover with hot water. Leave to soak for 10 minutes, or until softened. Drain and squeeze dry, then discard the hard centre stem and chop the mushrooms finely.

2   Combine the cornflour with ¹/₄ cup (60 ml/2 fl oz) water and mix to a fine paste. Add the soy sauce, oyster sauce and mirin.

3   Cook the noodles in a large pan of boiling salted water for 1–2 minutes, or according to the manufacturer's instructions. Drain and set aside.

4   Heat the wok until very hot, add the sesame oil and 1 tablespoon of the oil, and swirl it around to coat the side. Stir-fry the garlic, ginger and chicken strips in batches over high heat for 2–3 minutes, or until the chicken has cooked through. Remove from the wok and set aside.

5   Reheat the wok, add 1 tablespoon of the oil and stir-fry the red onion and spring onion for 1–2 minutes, or until softened. Add the dried and field mushrooms, then stir-fry the mixture for 1–2 minutes, or until tender. Remove from the wok and set aside.

6   Add the soy sauce mixture to the wok and stir for 1–2 minutes, or until the sauce is well heated and slightly thickened. Return the chicken and vegetables to the wok with the bean sprouts, noodles and mint. Stir until well coated with sauce. Serve at once.

INGREDIENTS

3 teaspoons Sichuan pepper
500 g (1 lb) chicken thigh fillets, cut into strips
2 tablespoons soy sauce
1 clove garlic, crushed
1 teaspoon grated fresh ginger
3 teaspoons cornflour (cornstarch)
100 g (3½ oz) dried thin egg noodles
oil, for cooking
1 onion, sliced
1 yellow capsicum (pepper), cut into thin strips
1 red capsicum (pepper), cut into thin strips
100 g (3½ oz) sugar snap peas
¼ cup (60 ml/2 fl oz) chicken stock

1 Heat the wok until very hot and dry-fry the Sichuan pepper for 30 seconds. Remove from the wok and crush with a mortar and pestle or in a spice mill or small food processor.

2 Combine the chicken pieces with the soy sauce, garlic, ginger, cornflour and Sichuan pepper in a bowl. Cover and refrigerate for 2 hours.

3 Cook the egg noodles in boiling water for 5 minutes, or until tender. Drain, then drizzle with a little oil and toss it through the noodles to prevent them from sticking together. Set aside.

4 Heat the wok until very hot, add 1 tablespoon of the oil and swirl it around to coat the side. Stir-fry the chicken in batches over medium-high heat for 5 minutes, or until golden brown and cooked. Add more oil when necessary. Remove from the wok and set aside.

5 Reheat the wok, add 1 tablespoon of the oil and stir-fry the onion, capsicum and sugar snap peas over high heat for 2–3 minutes, or until the vegetables are tender. Add the chicken stock and bring to the boil.

6 Return the chicken and egg noodles to the wok and toss over high heat. Serve immediately.

CHILLI BEEF

60 ml ('/₄ cup) kecap manis
2¹/₂ teaspoons sambal oelek
2 garlic cloves, crushed
¹/₂ teaspoon ground coriander (cilantro)
1 tablespoon grated palm sugar or soft brown sugar
1 teaspoon sesame oil
400 g (14 oz) beef fillet, partially frozen, thinly sliced
1 tablespoon peanut oil
2 tablespoons chopped roasted peanuts
3 tablespoons chopped coriander (cilantro) leaves

1   Combine the kecap manis, sambal oelek, garlic, ground coriander, palm sugar, sesame oil and 2 tablespoons water in a large bowl. Add the beef slices and coat well. Cover with plastic wrap and refrigerate for 20 minutes.

2   Heat a wok over high heat, add the peanut oil and swirl to coat. Add the meat in batches and cook each batch for 2–3 minutes, or until browned.

3   Arrange the beef on a serving platter, sprinkle with the chopped peanuts and coriander and serve with steamed rice.

INGREDIENTS

1 tablespoon cornflour (cornstarch)
2 teaspoons finely chopped ginger
2 garlic cloves, crushed
1 small red chilli, finely chopped
1 teaspoon sesame oil
60 ml (¼ cup) light soy sauce
500 g (1 lb 2 oz) chicken breast fillet, thinly sliced
1 tablespoon peanut oil
1 onion, halved and thinly sliced
115 g (4 oz) baby corn, halved on the diagonal
425 g (15 oz) baby bok choy (pak choi), trimmed and quartered lengthwise
2 tablespoons oyster sauce
60 ml (¼ cup) chicken stock

1 Combine half the cornflour with the ginger, crushed garlic, chilli, sesame oil and 2 tablespoons soy sauce in a large bowl. Add the chicken, toss until well coated and marinate for 10 minutes.

2 Heat a wok over high heat, add the peanut oil and swirl to coat. Stir-fry the onion for 2 minutes, or until soft and golden. Add the chicken in two batches and stir-fry for 5 minutes, or until almost cooked through. Add the baby corn and stir-fry for a further 2 minutes, then add the bok choy and cook for 2 minutes, or until wilted.

3 Mix the remaining soy sauce and cornflour with the oyster sauce and chicken stock in a small bowl, add to the wok and stir-fry for 1–2 minutes, or until the sauce has thickened to coating consistency and the chicken is cooked. Serve immediately with steamed rice or noodles.

INGREDIENTS

2 tablespoons oil
1 clove garlic, crushed
10 cm (4 inch) piece fresh ginger, peeled and thinly sliced
3 chicken breast fillets, sliced
4 spring onions, sliced
200 g (6$\frac{1}{2}$ oz) fresh asparagus spears, cut into short lengths
2 tablespoons soy sauce
$\frac{1}{3}$ cup (30 g/1 oz) slivered almonds, roasted

1 Heat a wok over high heat, add the oil and swirl to coat the side. Add the garlic, ginger and chicken and stir-fry for 1–2 minutes, or until the chicken changes colour.

2 Add the spring onion and asparagus and stir-fry for a further 2 minutes, or until the spring onion is soft.

3 Stir in the soy sauce and $\frac{1}{4}$ cup (60 ml/2 fl oz) water, cover and simmer for 2 minutes, or until the chicken is tender and the vegetables are slightly crisp. Sprinkle with the almonds and serve immediately.

INGREDIENTS

1 tablespoon oil
2 chicken breast fillets, cut into strips
2$\frac{1}{2}$ teaspoons seasoned peppercorns (see note)
1 onion, cut into wedges
1 red capsicum (pepper), cut into strips
2 tablespoons oyster sauce
1 teaspoon soy sauce
1 teaspoon sugar

1 Heat a wok over high heat, add the oil and swirl to coat the base and side of the wok. Add the chicken strips and stir-fry for 2–3 minutes, or until they are browned.

2 Add the peppercorns and stir-fry until they are fragrant. Add the onion and capsicum and stir-fry for 2 minutes, or until the vegetables have softened slightly.

3 Reduce the heat and stir in the oyster sauce, soy and sugar. Toss well to thoroughly combine before serving.

NOTE Seasoned peppercorns are available in the herb and spice section of large supermarkets.

PEPPERED CHICKEN

INGREDIENTS

1 tablespoon oil
700 g (1 lb 6 oz) minced (ground) chicken
2 cloves garlic, finely chopped
100 g (3½ oz) can water chestnuts, drained, chopped
1½ tablespoons oyster sauce
3 teaspoons soy sauce
1 teaspoon sugar
5 spring onions, finely sliced
4 lettuce leaves

1 Heat a wok over high heat, add the oil and swirl to coat the base and side of the wok. Add the chicken mince and garlic and stir-fry for 3–4 minutes, or until browned and cooked through, breaking up any lumps with the back of a spoon. Pour off any excess liquid.

2 Reduce the heat and add the water chestnuts, oyster sauce, soy sauce, sugar and spring onion.

3 Trim the lettuce leaves around the edges to neaten them and to form each one into a cup shape. Divide the chicken mixture among the lettuce cups and serve hot, with extra oyster sauce if you like.

Serves 4

INGREDIENTS

2 tablespoons sesame seeds
3 tablespoons light olive oil
10 chicken thigh fillets, cut into small pieces
3 teaspoons grated fresh ginger
1 teaspoon grated orange rind
$^1/_2$ cup (125 ml/4 fl oz) chicken stock
2 teaspoons honey
1 bunch (500 g/1 lb) bok choy, trimmed and halved

1 Toast the sesame seeds by dry-frying them in the wok, placing under a hot grill, or roasting them in a 200°C (400°F/Gas 6) oven for 5 minutes on a baking tray.

2 Heat a wok over high heat, add the oil and swirl to coat the base and side of the wok with oil. Add the chicken, in batches, and stir-fry for 3–4 minutes, or until golden.

3 Return all the chicken to the wok, add the ginger and orange rind, and cook for 20 seconds, or until fragrant. Add the stock and the honey and stir to combine. Increase the heat and cook for 3–4 minutes, or until the sauce has thickened slightly.

4 Add the bok choy to the wok and cook until it has slightly wilted. Season with salt and black pepper. Sprinkle with the toasted sesame seeds and serve immediately.

ASIAN GREENS WITH TERIYAKI TOFU DRESSING

650 g (1 lb 5 oz) baby bok choy
500 g (1 lb) choy sum
440 g (14 oz) snake beans, topped and tailed
¼ cup (60 ml/2 fl oz) oil
1 onion, thinly sliced
⅓ cup (60 g/2 oz) soft brown sugar
½ teaspoon ground chilli
2 tablespoons grated fresh ginger
1 cup (250 ml/8 fl oz) teriyaki sauce
1 tablespoon sesame oil
600 g (1¼ lb) silken firm tofu, drained

1 Cut the the baby bok choy and choy sum widthways into thirds. Cut the beans into 10 cm (4 inch) lengths.

2 Heat a wok over high heat, add 1 tablespoon of the oil and swirl to coat the side. Cook the onion in batches for 3–5 minutes, or until crisp. Remove with a slotted spoon and drain on paper towels.

3 Heat 1 tablespoon of the oil in the wok, add half the greens and stir-fry for 2–3 minutes, or until wilted. Remove and keep warm. Repeat with the remaining oil and greens. Remove. Drain any liquid from the wok.

4 Add the combined sugar, chilli, ginger and teriyaki sauce to the wok and bring to the boil. Simmer for 1 minute. Add the sesame oil and tofu and simmer for 2 minutes, turning once—the tofu will break up. Divide the greens among serving plates, then top with the dressing. Sprinkle with the fried onion.

INGREDIENTS

1 tablespoon sesame oil

2½ cups (500 g/1 lb) jasmine rice

2 tablespoons sesame oil, extra

1 long red chilli, seeded and finely chopped

2 cm (¾ inch) piece of fresh ginger, peeled and grated

2 cloves garlic, crushed

375 g (12 oz) green beans, cut into short lengths

½ cup (125 ml/4 fl oz) hoisin sauce

1 tablespoon soft brown sugar

2 tablespoons mirin

250 g (8 oz) tamari roasted almonds, roughly chopped (see note)

1 Preheat the oven to moderately hot 200°C (400°F/Gas 6). Heat the oil in a 1.5 litre (48 fl oz) ovenproof dish. Add the rice and stir to coat with oil. Stir in 1 litre (32 fl oz) boiling water. Cover and bake for 20 minutes, or until all the water is absorbed. Keep warm.

2 Meanwhile, heat the extra oil in a wok or large frying pan and cook the chilli, ginger and garlic for 1 minute, or until lightly browned. Add the beans, hoisin sauce and sugar and stir-fry for 2 minutes. Stir in the mirin and cook for 1 minute, or until the beans are tender but still crunchy.

3 Remove from the heat and stir in the almonds. Serve on a bed of the rice.

NOTE Tamari roasted almonds are available from health-food stores.

TAMARI ROASTED ALMONDS WITH SPICY GREEN BEANS

TEMPEH STIR-FRY

INGREDIENTS

1 teaspoon sesame oil
1 tablespoon peanut oil
2 cloves garlic, crushed
1 tablespoon grated fresh ginger
1 red chilli, finely sliced
4 spring onions, sliced on the diagonal
300 g (10 oz) tempeh, diced
500 g (1 lb) baby bok choy leaves
800 g (1 lb 10 oz) Chinese broccoli, chopped
½ cup (125 ml/4 fl oz) mushroom oyster sauce
2 tablespoons rice vinegar
2 tablespoons fresh coriander (cilantro) leaves
3 tablespoons toasted cashew nuts

1 Heat the oils in a wok over high heat, add the garlic, ginger, chilli and spring onion and cook for 1–2 minutes, or until the onion is soft. Add the tempeh and cook for 5 minutes, or until golden. Remove and keep warm.

2 Add half the greens and 1 tablespoon water to the wok and cook, covered, for 3–4 minutes, or until wilted. Remove and repeat with the remaining greens and more water.

3 Return the greens and tempeh to the wok, add the sauce and vinegar and warm through. Top with the coriander and nuts. Serve with rice.

INGREDIENTS

1 small Chinese cabbage, finely shredded
2 tablespoons oil
2 onions, halved and sliced thinly
500 g (1 lb) chicken thigh fillets, trimmed and cut into strips
$^1/_4$ cup (60 g/2 oz) sugar
$^1/_4$ cup (60 ml/2 fl oz) fish sauce
$^1/_3$ cup (80 ml/2$^3/_4$ fl oz) lime juice
1 tablespoon white vinegar
$^2/_3$ cup (30 g/1 oz) chopped Vietnamese mint or common mint
$^2/_3$ cup (30 g) chopped coriander (cilantro)
Vietnamese mint leaves, extra, to garnish

1   Place the cabbage in a large bowl, cover with plastic wrap and chill.

2   Heat a wok until very hot, add 1 tablespoon oil and swirl to coat. Add half the onion and half the chicken, and stir-fry for 4–5 minutes, or until the chicken is cooked through. Remove and repeat with the remaining oil, onion and chicken. Cool.

3   To make the dressing, mix together the sugar, fish sauce, lime juice, vinegar and $^1/_2$ teaspoon salt with a fork. To serve, toss together the cabbage, chicken and onion, dressing, mint and coriander and garnish with the mint leaves.

VIETNAMESE CHICKEN SALAD

QUICK THAI CHICKEN

1 tablespoon red curry paste

2 tablespoons oil

2 tablespoons fish sauce

2 tablespoons lime juice

$^1/_4$ cup (15 g/$^1/_2$ oz) chopped coriander (cilantro) leaves

1 tablespoon grated fresh ginger

1 teaspoon caster sugar

1 teaspoon sesame oil

750 g (1$^1/_2$ lb) chicken thigh fillets, cut into strips

1 tablespoon oil, extra

10 spring onions, cut into short lengths

100 g (3$^1/_2$ oz) snow peas (mangetout), trimmed

1 Whisk together the curry paste, oil, fish sauce, lime juice, coriander, ginger, sugar and sesame oil in a large non-metallic bowl. Add the chicken strips and toss to coat thoroughly.

2 Heat the extra oil in a wok. Add the chicken in batches and stir-fry for 3–5 minutes, or until browned all over, then remove from the wok and set aside. Add the spring onion and snow peas and stir-fry for 2 minutes. Return the chicken and any juices to the wok and stir-fry for 2–3 minutes, or until the chicken is heated through. Season with salt and pepper and serve.

INGREDIENTS

300 g (10¹/₂ oz) rump steak
1 garlic clove, crushed
3 tablespoons oyster sauce
2 teaspoons sugar
2 tablespoons soy sauce
5 tablespoons black bean sauce
2 teaspoons cornflour (cornstarch)
³/₄ teaspoon sesame oil
1.2 kg (2 lb 11 oz) fresh or 600 g (1 lb 5 oz) dried flat rice noodles
1¹/₂ tablespoons oil
2 red capsicums (peppers), sliced
1 green capsicum (pepper), sliced
a handful coriander (cilantro) leaves

1 Cut the steak across the grain into thin slices and put it in a bowl with the garlic, oyster sauce, sugar, soy sauce, black bean sauce, cornflour and sesame oil. Mix everything together, making sure the slices are all well coated.

2 If you are using dried rice noodles, soak them in boiling water for 10 minutes, or until they are opaque and soft. If your noodles are particularly dry, they may need a little longer. Drain the noodles.

3 Heat the oil in a wok or frying pan and, when it is hot, add the capsicums. Stir-fry the capsicums for a minute or two until they are starting to soften, then add the meat mixture and cook for a minute. Add the noodles and toss everything together well. Keep cooking until the meat is cooked through and everything is hot, then toss in the coriander leaves and stir once before turning off the heat. Serve straight away.

RICE NOODLES WITH BEEF, BLACK BEANS AND CAPSICUMS

COLOURFUL CABBAGE STIR-FRY

200 g (6^1/$_2$ oz) red cabbage
200 g (6^1/$_2$ oz) white cabbage
200 g (6^1/$_2$ oz) green cabbage
1 apple
oil, for cooking
1 teaspoon soft brown sugar
1 red onion, thinly sliced
1 red chilli, finely chopped
1 tablespoon chopped fresh thyme
1 tablespoon cider vinegar
^{2}/$_3$ cup (100 g/3^1/$_2$ oz) chopped blanched almonds

1 Finely shred the three different varieties of cabbage. Wash thoroughly, drain and dry well in a tea towel. Core and slice the apple.

2 Heat the wok until very hot, add 1 tablespoon of the oil and swirl it around to coat the side. Add the apple and brown sugar, and stir-fry for 1–2 minutes, or until the apple caramelizes. Remove the apple from the wok and set aside.

3 Reheat the wok, add a little oil if necessary and stir-fry the sliced red onion for 1 minute. Add the chopped chilli, shredded red cabbage and white cabbage, and stir-fry for 2–3 minutes. Add the shredded green cabbage and stir-fry for 1 minute. Stir in the thyme and the caramelized apple, and season well. Pour in the cider vinegar, cover and steam for 1 minute. Add the almonds and toss well until evenly distributed. Serve immediately.

INGREDIENTS

500 g (1 lb) squid tubes
1 tablespoon finely chopped fresh ginger
2–3 teaspoons finely chopped red chilli
3 cloves garlic, finely chopped
¼ cup (60 ml/2 fl oz) oil
2 onions, thinly sliced
500 g (1 lb) baby bok choy, roughly chopped

1 Wash the squid well and dry with paper towels. Cut into 1 cm (½ inch) rings and place in a bowl with the ginger, chilli, garlic and oil. Toss well. Cover and refrigerate for 2–3 hours.

2 Heat the wok until very hot and stir-fry the squid rings over high heat in three batches for 1–2 minutes, reserving the marinade. Remove from the wok as soon as the squid turns white. Keep the wok very hot and don't cook the squid for too long or it will toughen. Remove all the squid from the wok.

3 Pour the reserved marinade into the wok and bring to the boil. Add the onion and cook over medium heat for 3–4 minutes, or until slightly softened. Add the bok choy, cover and steam for 2 minutes, or until wilted. Add the squid and toss. Serve immediately.

MARINATED CHILLI SQUID

SALMON WITH LEEK AND CAMEMBERT IN HONEY MUSTARD SAUCE

500 g (1 lb) salmon fillet, cut into thick strips
¼ cup (60 g/2 oz) wholegrain mustard
1 tablespoon lime juice
2 tablespoons oil
1 leek, white part only, julienned
2 tablespoons tamari
2 teaspoons fish sauce
1 tablespoon honey
75 g (2½ oz) snow pea (mangetout) sprouts
½ cup (15 g/½ oz) coriander (cilantro) leaves, plus extra to
 garnish
100 g (3½ oz) Camembert, sliced
lime wedges, to serve

1 Place the salmon strips in a glass or ceramic bowl. Add the mustard and lime juice and toss to coat the salmon.

2 Heat the wok until very hot, add the oil and swirl it around to coat the side. Stir-fry the salmon in batches over high heat until it is slightly browned. Remove from the wok.

3 Add 1 tablespoon water to the wok, then add the leek and stir-fry until it is golden brown. Return the salmon to the wok, with the tamari, fish sauce and honey. Cook until the salmon is heated through.

4 Remove the wok from the heat and toss the snow pea sprouts and coriander leaves through the salmon. Serve topped with the Camembert and extra coriander, and the lime wedges on the side.

INGREDIENTS

1¹/₂ tablespoons oil
8 spring onions (scallions), cut into pieces
3 garlic cloves, crushed
8 cm (3 in) piece ginger, finely shredded
2 skinless chicken breasts, cut into strips
2 red capsicums (peppers), cut into strips
150 g (5¹/₂ oz) snow peas (mangetout)
100 g (3¹/₂ oz) cashews
2 tablespoons soy sauce
1¹/₂ teaspoons sesame oil

1 Heat the oil in a wok until it is smoking — this will only take a few seconds. Add the spring onion, garlic and ginger and stir them around for a few seconds. Next, add the chicken and stir it around until it has all turned white. Add the red capsicum and keep stirring, then throw in the snow peas and cashews and stir-fry for another minute or so.

2 Once the red capsicum has started to soften a little, add the soy sauce and sesame oil, toss everything together and then tip the stir-fry out into a serving dish.

3 Serve with rice or noodles and more soy sauce if you like.

STIR-FRIED CHICKEN WITH GINGER AND CASHEWS

INGREDIENTS

1 kg (2 lb) small eggplants (aubergine)
1 tablespoon salt
olive oil, for cooking
8 spring onions, sliced
3 cloves garlic, crushed
2 teaspoons cumin seeds
1 tablespoon ground coriander (cilantro)
1 teaspoon grated lemon rind
$^1/_3$ cup (80 ml/2$^3/_4$ fl oz) lemon juice
2 teaspoons soft brown sugar
2 tablespoons fresh coriander (cilantro) leaves

1 Peel the eggplants and cut into small cubes. Put in a colander and sprinkle with the salt. Leave for 30 minutes, then rinse under cold water and pat dry with paper towels.

2 Heat the wok until very hot, add 1$^1/_2$ tablespoons of the oil and swirl it around to coat the side. Stir-fry the eggplant in two batches over high heat for 3–4 minutes, or until browned and cooked (use 1$^1/_2$ tablespoons oil for each batch). Remove from the wok.

3 Return all the eggplant to the wok and add the spring onion. Stir-fry for 1 minute, or until the eggplant is soft. Add the garlic and cumin seeds, and cook for 1 minute. Stir in the ground coriander and cook for 30 seconds. Add the lemon rind, juice and sugar, and toss well. Season with salt and black pepper and sprinkle with coriander leaves. Delicious served with buckwheat noodles.

INGREDIENTS

Yellow curry paste
8 small dried red chillies
1 teaspoon black peppercorns
2 teaspoons coriander (cilantro) seeds
2 teaspoons cumin seeds
1 teaspoon ground turmeric
1¹/₂ tablespoons chopped galangal
5 garlic cloves, chopped
1 teaspoon grated ginger
5 red Asian shallots, chopped
2 stems lemon grass, white part only, chopped
1 teaspoon shrimp paste
1 teaspoon finely chopped lime zest

2 tablespoons peanut oil
500 ml (2 cups) coconut cream
125 ml (¹/₂ cup) vegetable stock
150 g (5¹/₂ oz) snake beans, cut into 3 cm (1¹/₄ inch) lengths
150 g (5¹/₂ oz) fresh baby corn
1 slender eggplant (aubergine), cut into 1 cm (¹/₂ inch) slices
100 g (3¹/₂ oz) cauliflower, cut into small florets
2 small zucchini (courgettes), cut into 1 cm (¹/₂ inch) slices
1 small red capsicum (pepper), cut into 1 cm (¹/₂ inch) slices
1¹/₂ tablespoons fish sauce
1 teaspoon grated palm sugar or soft brown sugar
1 small red chilli, chopped, to garnish
coriander (cilantro) leaves, to garnish

1   To make the curry paste, soak the chillies in boiling water for 15 minutes. Drain and chop them. Heat a frying pan, add the peppercorns, coriander seeds, cumin seeds and turmeric and dry-fry over medium heat for 3 minutes. Transfer to a mortar or food processor and pound or grind to a fine powder.

2   Using the mortar and pestle, pound the ground spices, chilli, galangal, garlic, ginger, shallots, lemon grass and shrimp paste until smooth. Stir in the lime zest.

3   Heat a wok over medium heat, add the oil and swirl to coat the side. Add 2 tablespoons of the curry paste and cook for 1 minute. Add 250 ml (1 cup) of the coconut cream. Cook over medium heat for 10 minutes, or until thick and the oil separates.

4   Add the chicken stock, the vegetables and remaining coconut cream and cook for 5 minutes, or until the vegetables are tender, but still crisp. Stir in the fish sauce and sugar. Garnish with the chilli and coriander.

INGREDIENTS

2 teaspoons Sichuan pepper

750 g (1½ lb) raw prawns (shrimp) , peeled and deveined,
    tails intact

2 tablespoons grated fresh ginger

3 cloves garlic, finely chopped

2 tablespoons Chinese rice wine or dry sherry

oil, for cooking

2 eggs, lightly beaten

½ red capsicum (pepper), cut into strips

½ green capsicum (pepper), cut into strips

4 spring onions, cut into pieces

100 g (3½ oz) snow peas (mangetout)

½ teaspoon salt

75 g (2½ oz) roasted unsalted peanuts, roughly chopped

50 g (1¾ oz) snow pea (mangetout) sprouts

1   Heat the wok until very hot and dry-fry the Sichuan pepper until it is fragrant. Remove from the wok and crush with a mortar and pestle or in a spice grinder.

2   Combine the prawns with the Sichuan pepper, ginger, garlic and wine in a glass or ceramic dish. Cover and refrigerate for 20 minutes.

3   Heat the wok until very hot, add 1½ tablespoons of the oil and swirl it around to coat the side. Dip three or four prawns in the beaten eggs, then stir-fry for about 1 minute, or until the prawns just change colour and are cooked. Remove from the wok. Repeat with the remaining prawns, reheating the wok to very hot for each batch and adding a little oil when needed. Remove the prawns from the wok.

4   Add the capsicum, spring onion, snow peas and salt to the wok. Stir-fry for 2 minutes, or until the vegetables are just crisp and tender.

5   Return the prawns to the wok with the peanuts and toss gently to combine. Serve immediately on a bed of snow pea sprouts.

INGREDIENTS

500 g (1 lb 2 oz) hokkien (egg) noodles
60 ml (¼ cup) peanut oil
20 scallops, roe and beards removed
1 large onion, cut into thin wedges
3 garlic cloves, crushed
1 tablespoon grated ginger
1 tablespoon chilli bean paste
150 g (5½ oz) choy sum, cut into 5 cm (2 inch) lengths
60 ml (¼ cup) chicken stock
2 tablespoons light soy sauce
2 tablespoons kecap manis
15 g (½ cup) coriander (cilantro) leaves
90 g (1 cup) bean sprouts
1 long red chilli, seeded and finely sliced
1 teaspoon sesame oil
1 tablespoon Chinese rice wine

1 Place the hokkien noodles in a heatproof bowl, cover with boiling water and soak for 1 minute until tender and separated. Drain, rinse under cold water, then drain again.

2 Heat a wok over high heat, add 2 tablespoons of the peanut oil and swirl to coat the side of the wok. Add the scallops in batches and sear for 20 seconds each side, or until sealed. Remove, then wipe the wok clean. Add the remaining oil and swirl to coat. Stir-fry the onion for 2 minutes, or until softened. Add the garlic and ginger and cook for 30 seconds. Stir in the chilli bean paste and cook for 1 minute, or until fragrant.

3 Add the choy sum to the wok with the noodles, stock, soy sauce and kecap manis. Stir-fry for 2–3 minutes, or until the choy sum has wilted and the noodles have absorbed most of the liquid. Return the scallops to the wok, add the coriander, bean sprouts, chilli, sesame oil and rice wine, tossing gently until combined.

SEARED SCALLOPS WITH CHILLI BEAN PASTE

INGREDIENTS

2 tablespoons oil
1 kg (2 lb) raw king prawns (shrimp), peeled, deveined and butterflied, tails left intact
3–4 cloves garlic, finely chopped
5 cm (2 inch) piece fresh ginger, cut into matchsticks
2–3 small red chillies, seeded and finely chopped
6 coriander (cilantro) roots, finely chopped, plus a few leaves to garnish
8 spring onions, cut into short lengths
½ red capsicum (pepper), thinly sliced
2 tablespoons lemon juice
½ cup (125 ml/4 fl oz) white wine
2 teaspoons crushed palm sugar
2 teaspoons fish sauce

1   Heat the wok until very hot, add the oil and swirl to coat. Stir-fry the prawns, garlic, ginger, chilli and coriander root in two batches for 1–2 minutes over high heat, or until the prawns turn pink. Remove all the prawns from the wok and set aside.

2   Add the spring onion and capsicum to the wok. Cook over high heat for 2–3 minutes. Add the lemon juice, wine and palm sugar. Cook until the liquid has reduced by two thirds.

3   Add the prawns and sprinkle with fish sauce. Toss to heat through. Garnish with coriander to serve.

INGREDIENTS

$1/4$ cup (60 ml) oil
400 g rump steak, thinly sliced across the grain
227 g can sliced bamboo shoots, drained and rinsed
3 cloves garlic, crushed with $1/4$ teaspoon salt
2 tablespoons fish sauce
8 spring onions, cut into 4 cm lengths on the diagonal
$1/4$ cup (40 g) sesame seeds, toasted

1 Heat a wok over high heat, add 2 tablespoons of the oil and swirl. When the oil is hot, add the beef in two batches and stir-fry for 1 minute, or until it starts to turn pink. Remove and set aside.

2 Add an extra tablespoon of oil if necessary, then stir-fry the bamboo shoots for 3 minutes, or until starting to brown. Add the garlic, fish sauce and $1/4$ teaspoon salt and stir-fry for 2–3 minutes. Add the spring onion and stir-fry for 1 minute, or until starting to wilt. Return the beef to the wok, stir quickly and cook for 1 minute until heated through. Remove from the heat, toss with the sesame seeds and serve with rice.

BEEF AND BAMBOO SHOOTS

SPICY CHILLI PRAWNS

20–24 raw prawns (shrimp), unpeeled
crusty bread and lemon wedges, to serve

Marinade
1 small red onion, finely chopped
$^1/_2$ cup (125 ml/4 fl oz) olive oil
1 tablespoon grated lime or lemon rind
2–3 cloves garlic, crushed
$^1/_2$ cup (125 ml/4 fl oz) lime or lemon juice
2–3 small red chillies, seeded and finely chopped
1 tablespoon grated fresh ginger
1 stem lemon grass, white part only, finely chopped
1 teaspoon ground turmeric

1 Place the prawns in a large glass or ceramic bowl. Add the marinade ingredients and toss well. Cover and refrigerate overnight. Turn the prawns once or twice while marinating.

2 Drain the prawns, reserving the marinade. Heat the wok until very hot and stir-fry the prawns in three batches over high heat until they are pink and very crispy. Remove from the wok.

3 Pour the reserved marinade into the wok. Bring to the boil, then return the prawns to the wok and toss well. Season and serve immediately.

NOTE The whole prawn, including the cripsy shell, can be eaten. If you prefer, you can discard the prawn heads before marinating.

INGREDIENTS

3 bird's eye chillies, seeded and finely chopped
3 garlic cloves, crushed
2 tablespoons fish sauce
1 teaspoon grated palm sugar or soft brown sugar
2 tablespoons peanut or vegetable oil
400 g (14 oz) lean beef fillet, thinly sliced across the grain
150 g (5¹/₂ oz) snake beans, sliced into 3 cm (1¹/₄ inch) lengths
30 g (1 cup) Thai basil
thinly sliced bird's eye chilli, to garnish

1   Combine the chilli, garlic, fish sauce, palm sugar and 1 tablespoon of the oil in a
    large non-metallic bowl. Add the beef, toss well, then cover and marinate in the fridge
    for 2 hours.

2   Heat a wok to hot, add 2 teaspoons of the oil and swirl to coat. Stir-fry the beef in two
    batches over high heat for 2 minutes each batch, or until just browned. Remove from
    the wok.

3   Heat the remaining oil in the wok, then add the snake beans and 60 ml (¹/₄ cup) water
    and cook over high heat for 3–4 minutes, tossing regularly, until tender. Return the beef to
    the wok with the basil. Cook for a further 1–2 minutes, or until warmed through. Garnish
    with chilli and serve.

SPICY CELLOPHANE NOODLES WITH MINCED PORK

200 g (7 oz) minced (ground) pork
1 teaspoon cornflour (cornstarch)
1^1/$_2$ tablespoons light soy sauce
2 tablespoons Chinese rice wine
1 teaspoon sesame oil
150 g (5^1/$_2$ oz) cellophane noodles (mung bean vermicelli)
2 tablespoons oil
4 spring onions (scallions), finely chopped
1 garlic clove, crushed
1 tablespoon finely chopped ginger
2 teaspoons chilli bean sauce
185 ml (^{3}/$_4$ cup) chicken stock
^{1}/$_2$ teaspoon sugar
2 spring onions (scallions), green part only, extra, thinly sliced on the diagonal

1 Combine the mince, cornflour, 1 tablespoon of the soy sauce, 1 tablespoon of the rice wine and ^{1}/$_2$ teaspoon of the sesame oil in a bowl, using a fork or your fingers. Cover with plastic wrap and marinate for 10–15 minutes.

2 Meanwhile, place the noodles in a heatproof bowl, cover with boiling water and soak for 3–4 minutes, or until softened. Drain well.

3 Heat a wok over high heat, add the oil and swirl to coat. Cook the spring onion, garlic, ginger and chilli bean sauce for 10 seconds, then add the mince mixture and cook for 2 minutes, stirring to break up any lumps. Stir in the stock, sugar, ^{1}/$_2$ teaspoon salt, and the remaining soy sauce, rice wine and sesame oil.

4 Add the noodles to the wok and toss to combine. Bring to the boil, then reduce the heat to low and simmer, stirring occasionally, for 7–8 minutes, or until the liquid is almost completely absorbed. Garnish with the extra spring onion and serve.

INGREDIENTS

250 g (8 oz) thick dried rice stick noodles
oil, for cooking
3 stems lemon grass, white part only, very thinly sliced
1 tablespoon grated fresh ginger
4 spring onions, chopped
1/4 teaspoon green peppercorns in brine, crushed
750 g (1 1/2 lb) broccoli, cut into small florets
150 g (5 oz) asparagus, cut into short lengths
3 teaspoons sesame oil
1 teaspoon sugar
250 g (8 oz) cooked fresh crab meat
75 g (2 1/2 oz) garlic chives, chopped
2 tablespoons lemon juice

1   Soak the noodles in boiling water for 8 minutes, or until soft and tender. Drain, cool a little, then drizzle with 1/2 tablespoon of oil and mix in lightly with your fingertips to prevent them sticking together. Cover to keep warm.

2   Heat the wok until very hot, add 1 tablespoon of the oil and swirl it around to coat the side. Stir-fry the lemon grass, ginger and spring onion for 15 seconds. Add the peppercorns, broccoli and asparagus and stir-fry for 1 minute. Add the sesame oil and sugar, and cook, covered, for 1–2 minutes, or until the asparagus and broccoli are just tender. Add the crab meat and cook for 1–2 minutes, or until heated through.

3   Add the noodles, chives and lemon juice, and toss well. Season well with salt and pepper. Serve immediately.

CRAB WITH ASPARAGUS AND BROCCOLI

$^1/_2$ cup (80 g/3 oz) raw cashew nuts

$1^1/_4$ cups (250 g/9 oz) jasmine rice

2 garlic cloves, finely chopped

$1^1/_2$ tablespoons fish sauce

1 tablespoon sambal oelek

1 tablespoon peanut oil

1 kg (2 lb) raw medium prawns (shrimp), peeled and deveined with tails intact

2 teaspoons tamarind concentrate

$1^1/_2$ tablespoons grated palm sugar

350 g choy sum, cut into 10 cm lengths

1 Preheat the oven to moderate 180°C (350°F/Gas 4). Spread the cashews on a baking tray and bake for 5–8 minutes, or until light golden—watch carefully, as they burn easily.

2 Meanwhile, bring a large saucepan of water to the boil. Add the rice and cook for 12 minutes, stirring occasionally. Drain well.

3 Place the garlic, fish sauce, sambal oelek and toasted cashews in a blender or food processor, adding 2–3 tablespoons of water, if needed, and blend to a rough paste.

4 Heat a wok until very hot, add the oil and swirl to coat. Add the prawns, toss for 1–2 minutes, or until starting to turn pink. Remove from the wok. Add the cashew paste and stir-fry for 1 minute, or until it starts to brown slightly. Add the tamarind, sugar and about $^1/_3$ cup (80 ml) water, then bring to the boil, stirring well. Return the prawns to the wok and stir to coat. Cook for 2–3 minutes, or until the prawns are cooked through.

5 Place the choy sum in a paper-lined bamboo steamer and steam over a wok or saucepan of simmering water for 3 minutes, or until tender. Serve with the prawns and rice.

INGREDIENTS

3 teaspoons salted black beans, rinsed
1 tablespoon shredded fresh ginger
2 cloves garlic, chopped
1 tablespoon sugar
2 tablespoons oyster sauce
1 teaspoon soy sauce
2 teaspoons oil
1 small red chilli, seeded and thinly sliced
1.2 kg (2 lb 6 oz) black mussels, scrubbed, debearded
2 teaspoons cornflour (cornstarch)
4 spring onions, sliced on the diagonal
coriander leaves, to serve

1 Place the black beans, ginger, garlic, sugar, oyster sauce and soy sauce in a small bowl and mash with a fork.

2 Heat a wok over high heat, add the oil and swirl to coat the side. Add the chilli and stir-fry for 30 seconds, then add the black bean mixture and stir-fry for 1 minute, or until fragrant. Add the mussels and stir-fry for 3–5 minutes, or until they open. Discard any that do not open. Reduce the heat to low.

3 Place the cornflour and ½ cup (125 ml/4 fl oz) water in a bowl and stir until smooth. Add to the wok and bring to the boil, stirring until the sauce boils and thickens. Stir through the spring onion and coriander leaves.

NOTE When buying live mussels make sure they are fresh. Live mussels will have tightly closed shells—some may be slightly opened. Give the shells a tap and if they close this will indicate that they are still alive. Discard any with broken or cracked shells. Always buy extra to allow for the ones that are cracked or do not open during cooking.

INGREDIENTS

350 g beef fillet, partially frozen
100 g snow peas (mangetout)
600 g fresh Hokkien noodles
1 tablespoon peanut oil
1 large onion, cut into thin wedges
1 large carrot, thinly sliced on the diagonal
1 medium red capsicum (pepper), cut into thin strips
2 cloves garlic, crushed
1 teaspoon grated fresh ginger
200 g fresh shiitake mushrooms, sliced
$1/4$ cup (60 ml) oyster sauce
2 tablespoons light soy sauce
1 tablespoon soft brown sugar
$1/2$ teaspoon five-spice powder

1   Cut the steak into thin slices. Top and tail the snow peas and slice in half diagonally. Soak the noodles in a large bowl with enough boiling water to cover for 10 minutes.

2   Spray a large wok with oil spray and when very hot, cook the steak in batches until brown. Remove and keep warm.

3   Heat the peanut oil in the wok, and when very hot, stir-fry the onion, carrot and capsicum for 2–3 minutes, or until tender. Add the garlic, ginger, snow peas and shiitake mushrooms, and cook for another minute before returning the steak to the wok.

4   Separate the noodles with a fork, then drain. Add to the wok, tossing well. Combine the oyster sauce with the soy sauce, brown sugar, five-spice powder and 1 tablespoon water and pour over the noodles. Toss until warmed through, then serve.

INGREDIENTS

Tamarind sauce
1 tablespoon tamarind purée
1 tablespoon vegetable oil
1 onion, finely diced
2 tablespoons palm sugar or soft brown sugar
2 tablespoons tamari

500 g (1 lb 2 oz) hokkien (egg) noodles
4 beef fillet steaks (about 115 g/4 oz each)
2 tablespoons oil
3 garlic cloves, crushed
1 small chilli, seeded and diced
300 g (10½ oz) baby green beans, trimmed
100 g (3½ oz) sugar snap peas, trimmed
1 tablespoon mirin
15 g (¼ cup) finely chopped coriander (cilantro) leaves

1 To make the tamarind sauce, dilute the tamarind in 250 ml (1 cup) hot water. Heat the oil in a saucepan. Add the onion and cook over medium heat for 6–8 minutes, or until soft and golden. Add the palm sugar and stir until dissolved. Add the tamarind liquid and tamari and simmer for 5 minutes, or until thick.

2 Rinse the noodles in a colander with warm water to soften – separate with your hands. Drain.

3 Season the steaks with salt and freshly ground black pepper. Heat half the oil in a large frying pan. Add the steaks and cook on each side for 3–4 minutes, or until cooked to your liking. Remove from the pan and rest in a warm place.

4 Heat the remaining oil in a wok and cook the garlic and chilli over high heat for 30 seconds. Add the beans and peas and cook for 2 minutes. Stir in the mirin and coriander. Add the noodles and toss through to heat.

5 Divide the noodles among four plates. Top with the steak and drizzle with the tamarind sauce.

STIR-FRIED SCALLOPS WITH SUGAR SNAP PEAS

2 tablespoons oil

2 large cloves garlic, crushed

3 teaspoons finely chopped fresh ginger

300 g sugar snap peas

500 g scallops without roe, membrane removed

2 spring onions, cut into 2 cm (1 inch) lengths

$2^1/_2$ tablespoons oyster sauce

2 teaspoons soy sauce

$^1/_2$ teaspoon sesame oil

2 teaspoons sugar

1   Heat a wok over medium heat, add the oil and swirl to coat the surface of the wok. Add the garlic and ginger, and stir-fry for 30 seconds, or until fragrant.

2   Add the peas to the wok and cook for 1 minute, then add the scallops and spring onion and cook for 1 minute, or until the spring onion is wilted. Stir in the oyster and soy sauces, sesame oil and sugar and heat for 1 minute, or until warmed through. Serve with rice.

325 g (11^1/$_2$ oz) fresh flat egg noodles (5 mm/^{1}/$_4$ inch wide)

5 cloves garlic, peeled

3 red Asian shallots, chopped

1 small fresh red chilli, seeded and chopped

3 fresh coriander (cilantro) roots, chopped

2^1/$_2$ tablespoons peanut oil

500 g (1 lb) snake beans, cut into 4 cm (1^1/$_2$ inch) lengths

2^1/$_2$ tablespoons fish sauce

1^1/$_2$ tablespoons grated palm sugar

1 tablespoon kecap manis

1 tablespoon lime juice

1 tablespoon crisp fried onion flakes

1   Cook the noodles in a saucepan of boiling water for 1 minute, or until tender. Drain well.

2   Place the garlic, red Asian shallots, chilli and coriander roots in a mortar and pestle or small food processor and grind to a smooth paste—add a little water if necessary.

3   Heat a wok over high heat, add the oil and swirl to coat. Stir in the paste and cook for 1 minute, or until fragrant. Add the beans, stir-fry for 2 minutes, then reduce the heat to low, cover and steam for 2 minutes. Increase the heat to high, add the fish sauce, palm sugar and kecap manis and stir-fry for 1 minute. Toss the noodles through the bean mixture for 1–2 minutes, or until heated through. Drizzle with the lime juice. Divide among serving bowls. If you wish, serve with lime wedges and garnish with the crisp fried onion flakes and sliced chilli.

INGREDIENTS

500 g (1 lb 2 oz) firm tofu
3–4 tablespoons oil
2 garlic cloves, crushed
2 teaspoons grated ginger
2 tablespoons oyster sauce
2 tablespoons soy sauce
2 teaspoons sugar
8 oyster mushrooms, quartered
2 spring onions (scallions), cut into pieces
2 baby bok choy (pak choi), quartered
a large handful coriander (cilantro) leaves

1   Cut the tofu into bite-sized pieces. Heat a wok over a medium heat, add half the oil and heat until it is very hot and almost smoking. Cook half the tofu until golden brown on all sides, making sure you move it around gently or it will stick and break. Remove from the pan and repeat with the remaining oil and tofu. Return the tofu to the pan.

2   Add the garlic, ginger, oyster sauce, soy sauce and sugar, then toss until well combined. Add the oyster mushrooms, spring onion and bok choy, then simmer until the sauce has reduced a little and the spring onion and bok choy have softened slightly. Garnish with the coriander leaves.

INGREDIENTS

1 tablespoon peanut oil
2 cloves garlic, crushed
1 tablespoon finely grated fresh ginger
2 tablespoons finely chopped lemon grass, white part only
8 spring onions, cut into short lengths
1 kg (2 lb) raw prawns (shrimp), peeled, deveined, tails intact
2 tablespoons lime juice
1 tablespoon soft brown sugar
2 teaspoons fish sauce
$^1/_4$ cup (60 ml/2 fl oz) chicken stock
1 teaspoon cornflour (cornstarch)
500 g (1 lb) baby bok choy, cut in half lengthways
$^1/_4$ cup (15 g/$^1/_2$ oz) chopped mint

1   Heat a wok until very hot, add the oil and swirl to coat. Add the garlic, ginger, lemon grass and spring onion, and stir-fry for 1 minute, or until fragrant. Add the prawns and stir-fry for 2 minutes.

2   Place the lime juice, sugar, fish sauce, chicken stock and cornflour in a small bowl. Mix well, then add to the wok and stir until the sauce boils and thickens. Cook for a further 1–2 minutes, or until the prawns are pink and just tender.

3   Add the bok choy and stir-fry for 1 minute, or until wilted. Stir in the mint and serve.

LAMB WITH HOKKIEN NOODLES AND SOUR SAUCE

INGREDIENTS

450 g (1 lb) hokkien (egg) noodles (see note)
2 tablespoons vegetable oil
375 g (13 oz) lamb backstrap, thinly sliced against the grain
70 g (2^1/$_2$ oz) red Asian shallots, peeled and thinly sliced
3 garlic cloves, crushed
2 teaspoons finely chopped ginger
1 small red chilli, seeded and finely chopped
1^1/$_2$ tablespoons red curry paste
125 g (4^1/$_2$ oz) snow peas (mangetout), trimmed and cut in half on the diagonal
1 small carrot, julienned
125 ml (^{1}/$_2$ cup) chicken stock
15 g (^{1}/$_2$ oz) palm sugar, grated, or soft brown sugar
1 tablespoon lime juice
small whole basil leaves, to garnish

1   Put the noodles in a bowl, cover with boiling water and soak for 1 minute. Drain and set aside.

2   Heat 1 tablespoon of the oil in a wok and swirl to coat the side. Stir-fry the lamb in batches over high heat for 2–3 minutes, or until it just changes colour. Remove to a side plate.

3   Add the remaining oil, then the shallots, garlic, ginger and chilli and stir-fry for 1–2 minutes. Stir in the curry paste and cook for 1 minute. Add the snow peas, carrot and the lamb and combine. Cook over high heat, tossing often, for 1–2 minutes.

4   Add the stock, palm sugar and lime juice, toss to combine and cook for 2–3 minutes. Add the noodles and cook for 1 minute, or until heated through. Divide among serving bowls and garnish with the basil.

NOTE   Hokkien noodles are thick, fresh egg noodles that have been cooked and lightly oiled before packaging. They are usually sold vacuum packed.

INGREDIENTS

1½ cups (300 g/10½ oz) long-grain rice
3 cloves garlic, finely chopped
1 tablespoon grated fresh ginger
4 stems lemon grass (white part only), finely chopped
2½ tablespoons oil
600 g (21 oz) lean rump steak, trimmed and sliced thinly across the grain
1 tablespoon lime juice
1–2 tablespoons fish sauce
2 tablespoons kecap manis
1 large red onion, cut into small wedges
200 g (7 oz) green beans, sliced on the diagonal into 5 cm (2 inches) lengths

1 Bring a large saucepan of water to the boil. Add the rice and cook for 12 minutes, stirring occasionally. Drain well.

2 Meanwhile, combine the garlic, ginger, lemon grass and 2 teaspoons of the oil in a non-metallic bowl. Add the beef, then marinate for 10 minutes. Combine the lime juice, fish sauce and kecap manis.

3 Heat a wok until very hot, add 1 tablespoon oil and swirl to coat. Stir-fry the beef in batches for 2–3 minutes, or until browned. Remove from the wok.

4 Reheat the wok to very hot, heat the remaining oil, then add the onion and stir-fry for 2 minutes. Add the beans and cook for another 2 minutes, then return the beef to the wok. Pour in the fish sauce mixture and cook until heated through. Serve with the rice.

LEMON GRASS BEEF

INGREDIENTS

4 eggs
1 spring onion (scallion), chopped
$1/3$ cup (50 g/$1^3/_4$ oz) fresh or frozen peas (optional)
3 tablespoons oil
4 cups (740 g/26 oz) cooked long-grain rice

1   Beat the eggs with a pinch of salt and 1 teaspoon of the spring onion. Cook the peas in a pan of simmering water for 3 minutes if fresh or 1 minute if frozen.

2   Heat a wok over high heat, add the oil and heat until very hot. Reduce the heat, add the egg and lightly scramble. Add the rice before the egg is completely set. Increase the heat, then stir to separate the rice grains and break the egg into small bits. Add the peas and the remaining spring onion, and season with salt. Stir constantly for 1 minute.

INGREDIENTS

250 g (8 oz) tempeh
oil, for cooking
1 onion, cut into thin slices
150 g (5 oz) asparagus, cut into short lengths
1 large carrot, cut into thick matchsticks
125 g (4 oz) snow peas (mangetout), chopped
425 g (14 oz) can baby corn, drained
2 tablespoons sweet chilli sauce
2 tablespoons kecap manis
2 tablespoons dry sherry

1 Drain the tempeh, pat dry with paper towels and cut into bite-sized pieces for stir-frying.

2 Heat the wok until very hot, add 2 tablespoons of the oil and swirl it around to coat the side. Stir-fry the tempeh in batches until crisp. Remove from the wok and set aside.

3 Reheat the wok, add a little more oil if necessary and stir-fry the onion for 1 minute. Add the asparagus, carrot and snow peas, and stir-fry for 2–3 minutes, or until the vegetables are just tender.

4 Return the fried tempeh to the wok and add the baby corn, sweet chilli sauce, kecap manis and sherry. Bring to the boil, then reduce the heat and simmer for 2 minutes. Toss well until heated through and serve.

CHILLI TEMPEH

HOT AND SWEET CHICKEN

125 ml ($^1/_2$ cup/4 oz) rice vinegar
160 g ($^2/_3$ cup/5$^1/_2$ oz) caster (superfine) sugar
6 garlic cloves, crushed
a large pinch of chilli flakes
1 teaspoon ground coriander (cilantro)
1 teaspoon ground white pepper
2 bunches coriander (cilantro), finely chopped, including roots and stems
3 tablespoons olive oil
2 tablespoons lemon juice
8 boneless and skinless chicken thighs, cut in half
2 tablespoons caster (superfine) sugar, extra
2 tablespoons fish sauce
1 small cucumber, peeled and sliced

1 Put the vinegar and sugar in a small saucepan, bring to the boil, then turn down the heat and simmer for a minute. Take the mixture off the heat and add two crushed garlic cloves, the chilli flakes and a pinch of salt. Leave the dressing to cool.

2 Heat a small frying pan for a minute, add the ground coriander and white pepper and stir it around for a minute. This will make the spices more fragrant. Add the rest of the garlic, the fresh coriander and a pinch of salt. Add 2 tablespoons of the oil and all the lemon juice and mix to a paste. Rub this all over the chicken pieces.

3 Heat the rest of the oil in a wok, add the chicken and fry it on both sides for 8 minutes, or until it is cooked through. Sprinkle in the extra sugar and the fish sauce and cook for another minute or two until any excess liquid has evaporated and the chicken pieces are sticky. Serve the chicken with the sliced cucumber and some rice. Dress with the sauce.

INGREDIENTS

1¹/₂ tablespoons peanut oil
1 large onion, finely chopped
2 garlic cloves, finely chopped
2 x 2 cm (³/₄ x ³/₄ inch) piece ginger, shredded
500 g (1 lb 2 oz) chicken thigh fillets, trimmed and cut into 2 cm (³/₄ inch) pieces
175 g (6 oz) Chinese cabbage, shredded
1 carrot, julienned
200 g (7 oz) Chinese barbecued pork (char sui), cut into 5 mm (¹/₄ inch) thick pieces
3 teaspoons Chinese rice wine
2 teaspoons sugar
150 g (5¹/₂ oz) snow peas (mangetout), trimmed
375 ml (1¹/₂ cups) chicken stock
1 tablespoon light soy sauce
225 g (8 oz) pancit canton (or Chinese e-fu) noodles (see note)
1 lemon, cut into wedges

1   Heat a wok over high heat, add the oil and swirl to coat. Add the onion and cook for 2 minutes, then add the garlic and ginger and cook for 1 minute. Add the chicken and cook for 2–3 minutes, or until browned. Stir in the cabbage, carrot, pork, rice wine and sugar and cook for a further 3–4 minutes, or until the pork is heated and the vegetables are soft. Add the snow peas and cook for 1 minute. Remove the mixture from the wok.

2   Add the chicken stock and soy sauce to the wok and bring to the boil. Add the noodles and cook, stirring, for 3–4 minutes, or until soft and almost cooked through.

3   Return the stir-fry mixture to the wok and toss with the noodles for 1 minute, or until combined. Divide among four warmed serving dishes and garnish with lemon wedges.

NOTE   Pancit canton noodles are used mostly in the Philippines and China, where they are called 'birthday' or 'long-life' noodles — their length denotes a long life for those who eat them. These round cakes of pre-boiled, deep-fried noodles are delicate and break easily. They are available in Asian grocery stores.

INGREDIENTS

400 g (13 oz) flat rice-stick noodles
2 tablespoons peanut oil
2 eggs, lightly beaten
1 onion, cut into thin wedges
2 cloves garlic, crushed
1 small red capsicum (pepper), thinly sliced
100 g (3½ oz) deep-fried tofu puffs, cut into thin strips
6 spring onions, thinly sliced
½ cup (30 g/1 oz) chopped fresh coriander (cilantro) leaves
¼ cup (60 ml/2 fl oz) soy sauce
2 tablespoons lime juice
1 tablespoon soft brown sugar
2 teaspoons sambal oelek
1 cup (90 g/3 oz) bean shoots
3 tablespoons chopped roasted unsalted peanuts

1 Cook the noodles in a saucepan of boiling water for 5–10 minutes, or until tender. Drain and set aside.

2 Heat a wok over high heat and add enough peanut oil to coat the bottom and side. When smoking, add the egg and swirl to form a thin omelette. Cook for 30 seconds, or until just set. Roll up, remove and thinly slice.

3 Heat the remaining oil in the wok. Add the onion, garlic and capsicum and cook over high heat for 2–3 minutes, or until the onion softens. Add the noodles, tossing well. Stir in the omelette, tofu, spring onion and half the coriander.

4 Pour in the combined soy sauce, lime juice, sugar and sambal oelek, then toss to coat the noodles. Sprinkle with the bean shoots and top with roasted peanuts and the remaining coriander. Serve immediately.

INGREDIENTS

2 tablespoons peanut oil
400 g (13 oz) deep-fried tofu puffs, halved
4 tablespoons oyster sauce
2 tablespoons light soy sauce
2 tablespoon sweet chilli sauce
2 tablespoon honey
2 cloves garlic, crushed
12 baby corn, halved lengthways
500 g (1 lb) choy sum leaves, cut into short lengths

1   Heat a wok over high heat, add the oil and swirl to coat the side. Add the tofu puffs and stir-try for 2 minutes, or until crispy and golden.

2   Place the oyster sauce, soy sauce, sweet chilli sauce and honey in a small bowl and mix together well.

3   Add the garlic, baby corn and choy sum to the wok and pour in the combined sauce, along with $^{1}/_{4}$ cup (60 ml/2 fl oz) water. Stir-fry for 3–4 minutes, or until the leaves have just wilted. Serve immediately.

FRIED TOFU, CHOY SUM AND BABY CORN IN OYSTER SAUCE

STIR-FRIED LAMB WITH MINT, CHILLI AND SHANGHAI NOODLES

400 g (14 oz) Shanghai noodles
1 teaspoon sesame oil
2 tablespoons peanut oil
220 g ($^1/_2$ lb) lamb fillet, cut into thin strips
2 cloves garlic, crushed
2 fresh red chillies, seeded and finely sliced
1 tablespoon oyster sauce
2 teaspoons palm sugar
2 tablespoons fish sauce
2 tablespoons lime juice
$^1/_2$ cup (10 g/$^1/_3$ oz) fresh mint, chopped
lime wedges, to garnish

1 Cook the noodles in a large saucepan of boiling water for 4–5 minutes. Drain, then rinse in cold water. Add the sesame oil and toss through.

2 Heat the peanut oil in a wok over high heat. Add the lamb and cook in batches for 1–2 minutes, or until just browned. Return all the meat to the wok and add the garlic and chilli. Cook for 30 seconds then add the oyster sauce, palm sugar, fish sauce, lime juice and noodles. Cook for another 2–3 minutes, or until the noodles are warm. Stir in the mint and serve immediately with the lime wedges.

INGREDIENTS

2 tablespoons oil
3 Asian shallots, sliced
1 garlic clove, finely chopped
1 small red chilli, finely chopped
100 g (3½ oz) snake or green beans, cut into short pieces
1 small red capsicum (pepper), cut into batons
90 g (3¼ oz) button mushrooms, halved
470 g (2½ cups) cooked jasmine rice
1 teaspoon grated palm sugar
3 tablespoons light soy sauce
10 g (¼ cup) fresh Thai basil, shredded
1 tablespoon coriander (cilantro) leaves, chopped
fried red Asian shallot flakes, to garnish
Thai basil leaves, to garnish

1   Heat a wok over high heat, add the oil and swirl. Stir-fry the shallots, garlic and chilli for
    3 minutes, or until the shallots start to brown. Add the beans, capsicum and mushrooms,
    stir-fry for 3 minutes, or until cooked, then stir in the cooked jasmine rice and heat
    through.

2   Dissolve the palm sugar in the soy sauce, then pour over the rice. Stir in the herbs.
    Garnish with the shallot flakes and basil.

INGREDIENTS

2 garlic cloves, crushed

2 teaspoons grated ginger

1 teaspoon five-spice powder

1/4 teaspoon ground white pepper

2 tablespoons Chinese rice wine

1 teaspoon sugar

1 kg (2 lb 4 oz) boneless lamb shoulder, trimmed and cut
   into 3 cm (1 1/4 inch) pieces

30 g (1 oz) whole dried Chinese mushrooms

1 tablespoon peanut oil

1 large onion, cut into wedges

2 cm (3/4 inch) piece ginger, julienned

1 teaspoon Sichuan peppercorns, crushed or ground

2 tablespoons sweet bean paste

1 teaspoon black peppercorns, ground and toasted

500 ml (2 cups) chicken stock

60 ml (1/4 cup) oyster sauce

2 star anise

60 ml (1/4 cup) Chinese rice wine, extra

80 g (2 3/4 oz) can sliced bamboo shoots, drained

100 g (3 1/2 oz) can water chestnuts, drained and sliced

400 g (14 oz) fresh rice noodles, cut into 2 cm (3/4 inch)
   wide strips

1 spring onion (scallion), sliced on the diagonal

1 Combine the garlic, grated ginger, five-spice powder, white pepper, rice wine, sugar and 1 teaspoon salt in a large bowl. Add the lamb and toss to coat. Cover and marinate for 2 hours.

2 Meanwhile, soak the mushrooms in boiling water for 20 minutes. Drain. Discard the stems and slice the caps.

3 Heat a wok over high heat, add the oil and swirl to coat. Stir-fry the onion, julienned ginger and Sichuan pepper for 2 minutes. Cook the lamb in three batches, stir-frying for 2–3 minutes each batch, or until starting to brown. Stir in the bean paste and ground peppercorns and cook for 3 minutes, or until the lamb is brown. Add the stock and transfer to a 2 litre (8 cup) flameproof clay pot or casserole dish. Stir in the oyster sauce, star anise and extra rice wine and simmer, covered, over low heat for 1 hours, or until the lamb is tender. Stir in the bamboo shoots and water chestnuts and cook for 20 minutes. Add the mushrooms.

4 Cover the noodles with boiling water and gently separate. Drain and rinse, then add to the hotpot, stirring for 1–2 minutes, or until heated through. Sprinkle with the spring onion.

INGREDIENTS

20 stems Chinese broccoli
4 baby bok choy
100 g (3½ oz) shimeji or enoki mushrooms
100 g (3½ oz) shiitake mushrooms
1 tablespoon soy sauce
2 teaspoons crushed palm sugar
1 tablespoon oil
4 spring onions, cut into short pieces
5 cm (2 inch) fresh ginger, cut into thin strips
1–2 small red chillies, seeded and finely chopped
2–3 cloves garlic, crushed
125 g (4 oz) snow peas (mangetout), halved
1–2 teaspoons seasoning sauce

1 Remove any tough outer leaves from the Chinese broccoli and bok choy. Cut into 4 cm (1½ inch) pieces across the leaves, including the stems. Wash thoroughly, then drain and dry thoroughly. Wipe the mushrooms with a paper towel and trim the ends. Slice the shiitake mushrooms thickly.

2 Combine the soy sauce and palm sugar with ¼ cup (60 ml/2 fl oz) water. Set aside.

3 Heat the wok until very hot, add the oil and swirl it around to coat the side. Stir-fry the spring onion, ginger, chilli and garlic over low heat for 30 seconds, without browning. Increase the heat to high and add the Chinese broccoli, bok choy and snow peas. Stir-fry for 1–2 minutes, or until the vegetables are wilted.

4 Add the prepared mushrooms and soy sauce mixture. Stir-fry over high heat for 1–2 minutes, or until the mushrooms and sauce are heated through. Sprinkle with the seasoning sauce, to taste, and serve immediately.

INGREDIENTS

400 g (14 oz) fresh flat egg noodles (5 mm/^{1}/$_4$ inch wide)
2 tablespoons peanut oil
4 red Asian shallots, thinly sliced
2 garlic cloves, chopped
1 small red chilli, finely diced
200 g (7 oz) pork fillet, thinly sliced across the grain
200 g (7 oz) chicken breast fillet, thinly sliced
200 g (7 oz) small raw prawns (shrimp), peeled and deveined, with tails intact
2 Chinese cabbage leaves, shredded
2 carrots, cut in half lengthways and thinly sliced
100 g (3^1/$_2$ oz) snake beans, cut into 3 cm (1^1/$_4$ inch) lengths
60 ml (^{1}/$_4$ cup) kecap manis
1 tablespoon light soy sauce
2 tomatoes, peeled, seeded and chopped
4 spring onions (scallions), sliced on the diagonal
1 tablespoon crisp fried onion flakes
flat-leaf (Italian) parsley, to garnish

1 Cook the noodles in a large saucepan of boiling water for 1 minute, or until tender. Drain and rinse them under cold water.

2 Heat a wok over high heat, add the oil and swirl to coat. Stir-fry the Asian shallots for 30 seconds. Add the garlic, chilli and pork and stir-fry for 2 minutes, then add the chicken and cook a further 2 minutes, or until the meat is golden and tender.

3 Add the prawns and stir-fry for another 2 minutes, or until pink and just cooked. Stir in the cabbage, carrot and beans and cook for 3 minutes, then add the noodles and gently stir-fry for 4 minutes, or until heated through — taking care not to break up the noodles. Stir in the kecap manis, soy sauce, chopped tomato and spring onion and stir-fry for 1–2 minutes.

4 Season with salt and freshly ground black pepper. Garnish with the fried onion flakes and parsley.

NOTE This dish, called bahmi goreng in Indonesian, is traditionally eaten with chopped roasted peanuts and sambal oelek on the side. It is also delicious with satay sauce.

INGREDIENTS

2 tablespoons oil
300 g (10 oz) broccoli, cut into small florets
150 g (5 oz) snake beans, cut into short lengths
3 spring onions, sliced
250 g (8 oz) cabbage, finely shredded
1 green capsicum (pepper), cut into strips
2 tablespoons lime juice
1 tablespoon soft brown sugar
$1/4$ cup (15 g/$1/2$ oz) Thai basil, shredded

1 Heat the wok until very hot, add the oil and swirl it around to coat the side. Stir-fry the broccoli and snake beans for 3–4 minutes, or until the vegetables are bright green and just tender. Add the spring onion, cabbage and capsicum, and continue stir-frying until just softened.

2 Combine the lime juice and brown sugar, stirring until the sugar has dissolved. Add to the wok with the basil. Toss to combine with the vegetables and serve immediately.

NOTE You can include any suitable kind of green vegetable in this dish, including Asian greens. If you can't find Thai basil, use ordinary basil or coriander—either will give fragrance and flavour like Thai basil.

SWEET CHILLI PRAWNS

1 kg (2 lb) raw medium prawns (shrimp)
2 tablespoons peanut oil
1 cm x 3 cm ($^1/_2$ inch x 1 inch) piece fresh ginger, cut into julienne strips
2 cloves garlic, finely chopped
5 spring onions, cut into 3 cm lengths
$^1/_3$ cup (80 ml/2$^3/_4$ oz) chilli garlic sauce
2 tablespoons tomato sauce
2 tablespoons Chinese rice wine
1 tablespoon Chinese black vinegar or rice vinegar
1 tablespoon soy sauce
1 tablespoon soft brown sugar
1 teaspoon cornflour (cornstarch) mixed with $^1/_2$ cup (125 ml/4 oz) water
finely chopped spring onion, to garnish

1 Peel and devein the prawns, leaving the tails intact. Heat a wok until very hot, then add the oil and swirl to coat the side. Heat over high heat until smoking, then quickly add the ginger, garlic and spring onion and stir-fry for 1 minute. Add the prawns and cook for 2 minutes, or until they are just pink and starting to curl. Remove the prawns from the wok with tongs or a slotted spoon.

2 Put the chilli garlic sauce, tomato sauce, rice wine, vinegar, soy sauce, sugar and cornflour paste in a small jug and whisk together. Pour the sauce into the wok and cook, stirring, for 1–2 minutes, or until it thickens slightly. Return the prawns to the wok for 1–2 minutes, or until heated and cooked through. Garnish with the finely chopped spring onion. Serve immediately with rice or thin egg noodles.

NOTE Chinese rice wine has a rich sweetish taste. Use dry sherry if unavailable. Chinese black vinegar is made from rice and has a sweet, mild taste. It is available in Asian food stores.

INGREDIENTS

5 dried shiitake mushrooms
1 clove garlic, crushed
2 teaspoons grated fresh ginger
$^1/_2$ cup (125 ml/4$^1/_4$ fl oz) Japanese soy sauce
2 tablespoons rice wine vinegar
2 tablespoons sugar
1 tablespoon lemon juice
500 g (17$^1/_2$ oz) fresh udon noodles
2 tablespoons oil
500 g (17$^1/_2$ oz) chicken thigh fillets, thinly sliced
1 clove garlic, extra, finely chopped
1 small red capsicum (pepper), thinly sliced
2 cups (150 g/5$^1/_2$ oz) shredded cabbage
4 spring onions, thinly sliced
1 tablespoon sesame oil
white pepper, to taste
2 tablespoons drained shredded pickled ginger

1 Place the mushrooms in a heatproof bowl and soak in boiling water for 10 minutes, or until tender. Drain, reserving $^1/_4$ cup (60 ml) of the liquid. Discard the stems, squeeze the caps dry and thinly slice.

2 Combine the crushed garlic, ginger, soy sauce, vinegar, sugar, lemon juice and reserved soaking liquid.

3 Place the noodles in a heatproof bowl, cover with boiling water and leave for 2 minutes, or until soft and tender. Drain.

4 Heat a wok over high heat, add half the oil and swirl to coat. Add the chicken in batches and stir-fry for 5 minutes, or until browned. Remove from the wok.

5 Add the remaining oil and swirl to coat. Add the extra chopped garlic, mushrooms, capsicum and cabbage, and stir-fry for 2–3 minutes, or until softened. Add the noodles and stir-fry for another minute. Return the chicken to the wok and add the spring onion, sesame oil and soy sauce mixture, stirring until well combined and heated through. Season with white pepper and scatter with the pickled ginger.

SWEET PORK

850 g (30 oz) pork spareribs
$^1/_2$ cup (125 g/4$^1/_2$ oz) grated palm sugar or soft brown sugar
4 red Asian shallots, sliced
1 tablespoon fish sauce
1 tablespoon kecap manis
$^1/_2$ teaspoon white pepper
$^1/_3$ cup (10 g/$^1/_2$ oz) loosely packed fresh coriander (cilantro) leaves

1 Remove the bone and outer rind from the ribs. Cut into 1 cm ($^1/_2$ inch) slices.

2 Place the sugar in a wok with 2 tablespoons water and stir over low heat until the sugar dissolves. Increase to medium heat and boil, without stirring, for 5 minutes, or until the sugar turns an even, golden brown. Add the pork and shallots and stir to coat. Add the fish sauce, kecap manis, pepper and 1 cup (250 ml/8 fl oz) warm water. Stir until any hard bits of sugar have melted.

3 Cover and cook for 10 minutes, stirring occasionally, then cook, uncovered and stirring often, for 20–30 minutes, or until the sauce is sticky and the meat is cooked. Garnish with coriander and serve with rice.

All our recipes are thoroughly tested in a specially developed test kitchen. Standard metric measuring cups and spoons are used in the development of our recipes. All cup and spoon measurements are level. We have used 60 g (2¼ oz/Grade 3) eggs in all recipes. Sizes of cans vary from manufacturer to manufacturer and between countries – use the can size closest to the one suggested in the recipe.

CONVERSION GUIDE

1 cup = 250 ml (9 fl oz)

1 teaspoon = 5 ml

1 Australian tablespoon = 20 ml (4 teaspoons)

1 UK/US tablespoon = 15 ml (3 teaspoons)

DRY MEASURES	LIQUID MEASURES	LINEAR MEASURES
30 g = 1 oz	30 ml = 1 fl oz	6 mm = ¼ inch
250 g = 9 oz	125 ml = 4 fl oz	1 cm = ½ inch
500 g = 1 lb 2 oz	250 ml = 9 fl oz	2.5 cm = 1 inch

CUP CONVERSIONS – DRY INGREDIENTS

1 cup almonds, slivered whole = 125 g (4½ oz)

1 cup cheese, lightly packed processed cheddar = 155 g (5½ oz)

1 cup wheat flour = 125 g (4½ oz)

1 cup wholemeal flour = 140 g (5 oz)

1 cup minced (ground) meat = 250 g (9 oz)

1 cup pasta shapes = 125 g (4½ oz)

1 cup raisins = 170 g (6 oz)

1 cup rice, short grain, raw = 200 g (7 oz)

1 cup sesame seeds = 160 g (6 oz)

1 cup split peas = 250 g (9 oz)

INTERNATIONAL GLOSSARY

capsicum	sweet bell pepper
chick pea	garbanzo bean
chilli	chile, chili pepper
cornflour	cornstarch
eggplant	aubergine
spring onion	scallion
zucchini	courgette
plain flour	all-purpose flour
prawns	shrimp
minced meat	ground meat

Where temperature ranges are indicated, the lower figure applies to gas ovens, the higher to electric ovens. This allows for the fact that the flame in gas ovens generates a drier heat, which effectively cooks food faster than the moister heat of an electric oven, even if the temperature setting is the same.

	°C	°F	GAS MARK
Very slow	120	250	½
Slow	150	300	2
Mod slow	160	325	3
Moderate	180	350	4
Mod hot	190(g)–210(e)	375–425	5
Hot	200(g)–240(e)	400–475	6
Very hot	230(g)–260(e)	450–525	8

INDEX

Published in 2006 by Bay Books,
an imprint of Murdoch Books Pty Limited.

ISBN 1-74045-942-3
978-1-74045-942-6

Printed by Sing Cheong Printing Company Ltd.
Printed in China.

Copyright © Text, photography and illustrations Murdoch Books © 2006
All rights reserved. No part of this publication may be reproduced, stored in a retrieval system or
transmitted in any form or by any means, electronic, mechanical, photocopying, recording or
otherwise, without the prior written permission of the publisher.